Books by Janice Hardy

Foundations of Fiction
Plotting Your Novel: Ideas and Structure
Plotting Your Novel Workbook
Revising Your Novel: First Draft to Finished Draft Series
Book One: Fixing Your Character & Point-of-View Problems
Book Two: Fixing Your Plot & Story Structure Problems
Book Three: Fixing Your Setting & Description Problems

Skill Builders
Understanding Show, Don't Tell (And Really *Getting It)*
Understanding Conflict (And What It Really *Means)*

Novels
The Healing Wars Trilogy:
The Shifter
Blue Fire
Darkfall

As J.T. Hardy
Blood Ties

ISBN 978-0-9915364-8-1

UNDERSTANDING
Conflict

(And What It *Really* Means)

Learn how to create compelling conflict in your fiction

Janice Hardy

Fiction University's Skill Builders Series

Contents

26 Things That Affect Conflict

56 The Different Layers of Conflict

82 Common Reasons for Weak or No Conflict

101 Ways to Create Conflict in Your Manuscript

127 Go Cause Trouble!

129 Thanks!

130 More from Janice Hardy

133 Acknowledgments

135 About the Author

Welcome to *Understanding Conflict (And What It Really Means)*

Like most writers, I've spent countless hours creating conflict in my novels. I've thrown exciting obstacles in my protagonists' paths, I've developed sinister antagonists to thwart my heroes, I've devised cruel ways to put my characters through mental anguish—and my beta readers have *still* told me, "This book needs more conflict."

Because despite what we "know" about conflict as writers, the concept isn't so cut and dry.

It's not just about the obstacles in the path, or the bad guy with the evil plan, or the mental anguish of the hero. It's not the plot or the character arc, even though we often talk about it like it is. It's a tapestry woven from multiple aspects of writing that work together to create a feeling that victory will *not* come easily to the characters, and it leaves readers dying to know what the protagonist is going to do about it. Conflict can be confusing because:

- *Conflict* is more than one single thing.

- *Conflict* changes depending on who you talk to.

- *Conflict* changes depending on how you use it.

Conflict is a pain in the butt that makes us want to bash our heads against the keyboard on a regular basis, and even makes us want to curl up and cry in the corner. I've been there myself, I know how frustrating it can be, and I've put this book together to help my fellow writers avoid some of that frustration and keyboard-bashing.

Creating conflict isn't that hard once you figure out what it means and how it applies to your novel. Realizing it isn't a one-size-fits-all means you'll be able to find the right conflict to suit your need, no matter what that need is. You'll learn how to parse feedback and how to diagnose your own manuscripts to spot trouble areas before they become problems.

What You'll Get From This Book

Understanding Conflict (And What It Really *Means)* is an in-depth study and analysis of what conflict means and how to use it in your writing. It will help you understand the different layers of conflict and how they work together to create the problems and goals in your story, as well as explore the elements of writing that affect conflict, such as stakes and character motivations. It will discuss the common problems that result from a lack of conflict, and offer suggestions and tips on how to strengthen conflict in your story.

By the end of this book, you'll have a solid understanding of what conflict is and have the ability to create strong and compelling conflicts in your own novel.

What Conflict Really Means

Ask any agent or editor to list the top three reasons manuscripts get rejected and you'll find "not enough conflict" on that list. Conflict is at the core of every story, and without conflict, there is no story. It's so vital, "conflict" and "story" are almost interchangeable when writers talk about it. It's common to ask, "What's your story about?" and have the author describe the conflict.

Which is part of the problem.

Since conflict covers such a wide range of storytelling, it isn't always clear what people *mean* when they say "conflict." This can cause a lot of frustration—especially for new writers. Does it mean the plot of the story? The character arc? Does conflict mean the characters have to argue? Does it mean a physical battle? Does it mean soul-crushing angst or a mustached villain plotting against the hero at every turn?

No. Conflict fuels the plot and character arc, but they're separate elements. You can have conflict without battles, without major angst, and without evil villains bent on world domination. Some of the best conflicts are those between characters who love each other deeply, but can't agree on what to do about a problem.

I think the biggest reason writers struggle with conflict is that it's not just one thing. Conflict is a one-two combo of a challenge faced and the struggle to overcome that challenge.

- The conflict of the plot (the physical challenges faced to resolve the problem)

- The conflict of the character (the mental challenges faced to resolve the problem)

These are the two sides of conflict and they appear in every story (and scene) in some fashion. Let's look at each of them a little closer.

The Conflict of the Plot

A plot is external. It's what the protagonist does to resolve the problem of the novel (the core conflict). The plot's conflicts are also external, consisting of the individual challenges the protagonist faces on a scene-by-scene basis. Resolving these conflicts creates the plot and leads the protagonist from page one to the final page of the novel. Think of it like the to-do list for the novel. Follow this list of challenges to resolve the plot.

The conflict of the plot *is what's making it physically hard* for the protagonist to do what she has to do.

For example:

▶ To sneak into the building, the protagonist must find a way to disable the security cameras and locks—the conflict (challenge) is the technology and security people preventing her from entering the building.

▶ To catch the love interest's eye, the protagonist must attend a party she hasn't been invited to—the conflict (challenge) is her attempt to get into that party when she's being excluded.

▶ To defeat the two-headed troll, the protagonist must find a way to use her physical fighting skills and wits to win over a much stronger foe—the conflict (challenge) is overcoming her physical limits to best a monster that could easily squash her like a bug.

Real conflict involves opposition to a goal and the challenges to overcome that opposition.

However, when people refer to the plot's conflict in a scene, it's often the *goal* they're talking about—which is why writers can sometimes think their scene has conflict when it really doesn't. They're referring to what the protagonist has to do, not the challenge *to achieve* that goal. You might have a goal of emptying the dishwasher, but unless that task presents a challenge to complete it, it's not a conflict.

For example:

- ▶ The protagonist must sneak into a building and steal the plans.

- ▶ The protagonist must ask her love interest out on a date.

- ▶ The protagonist must defeat the two-headed troll intent on eating her.

These are all goals that could easily move a plot forward, but these "conflicts" are just tasks to be completed—there's no challenge associated with achieving them. Without something in the way of completing these tasks, they're nothing more than simple obstacles. The conflict (in the story sense of the word) is what's *preventing* the protagonist from completing her goal. Otherwise, the protagonist can just waltz in and accomplish her task with little to no resistance. No resistance (no challenge) = no conflict.

Test Your Conflict: One trick to test if you have an obstacle or a conflict is to put the scene in an "if-then" statement.

For example:

- ▶ If she can disable the security, then she can break into the building (protagonist vs. security).

- ▶ If she can steal an invitation from the printer, then she can get into the party (protagonist vs. staff at the print shop).

- ▶ If she can move fast enough, then she can defeat the troll (protagonist vs. physical weakness).

You can quickly see what specifically has to be done to accomplish the task, and judge if there's a challenge or struggle associated with that task. For conflicts that are just obstacles, these "if-then" statements usually read a little differently.

For example:

- ▶ If she can get into the building, then she can steal the plans (notice nothing is stated that shows how "get into the building" will be a challenge).

- ▶ If she can get an invitation, then she can go to the party (notice this is basically how parties work, so there's nothing to suggest this is a challenge for the protagonist).

- ▶ If she can be tougher and stronger, then she can defeat the troll (notice this is close to the original, but can the protagonist really be "tougher and stronger" than a troll three times her size?).

The key here is to find the specific task that must be done to accomplish the goal. If the task is basically "do it" in some way, odds are there's no conflict. Let's look at some conflicts that aren't really conflicts:

For example:

- ▶ If she can disable the security, then she can break into the building (except she's an expert thief and the security is so old she could have cracked it when she was 10. In this case, "disabling the security" is a form of "do it." All she has to do is complete this task and she succeeds, yet this task isn't a challenge at all).

- ▶ If she can steal an invitation from the printer, then she can get into the party (except she works at the print shop and handled the invitation job, and all she has to do is slip one in her pocket. Again, no challenge to the task preventing her from her goal, so no conflict).

- ▶ If she can move fast enough, then she can defeat the troll (except she has special powers that give her supernatural speed and strength when she most needs it. "Moving fast" is how she completes this task, and it's not a challenge to do it).

No matter how impressive a potential problem seems, if there's no challenge in overcoming it, it's not a strong story conflict.

A word of warning here: It's up to each writer to decide if the conflict is a challenge or not. You can have what seems like a solid conflict on paper, but when the scene is written, the challenge isn't hard to accomplish at all and the conflict feels weak to your readers.

The Conflict of the Character

A character conflict is internal. It's the emotional struggle the protagonist faces to resolve her challenges. These conflicts make it harder for the protagonist to make decisions, because choosing what to do has emotional consequences, and often, the right choice is the one the protagonist doesn't *want* to make.

The conflict of the character *is what's making it emotionally hard* for the protagonist to do what she has to do.

For example:

▶ In order to steal the plans, the protagonist needs to use (and reveal) the thieving skills she's been trying to keep secret from her new boyfriend. (She can't get the plans and keep her secret, so she has to choose which is more important to her.)

▶ In order to get into the party, the protagonist must use the connections of the family who disowned her (She can't meet her love interest without revealing the truth about her scandalous past, so she has to choose if love is worth the risk.)

▶ In order to defeat the troll, the protagonist must fight it in the middle of town where it has limited mobility. (She can't beat the troll in the open, so she has to choose how many lives she's willing to risk to stop a greater threat.)

The conflict of the character is the emotional struggle the protagonist faces while deciding what to do about the external problem. Risk the secret. Reveal the past. Endanger the innocent. It makes the protagonist ask, "Is this goal worth the price I'll have to pay to get it?" Sometimes the answer is yes, sometimes it's no, and sometimes the protagonist tries her best to get the goal without paying the price, which rarely goes well for her.

However, when people refer to the character conflict in a scene, it's often the *character arc* they're actually talking about—which is why writers can feel all character conflict (internal conflict) needs to result in character growth, but it really doesn't. You can have internal conflict without a character arc. The protagonist can struggle over the right choice without changing as a person.

For example:

▶ In order to steal the plans, the protagonist will have to struggle against exposing her criminal past. (Yet exposing that past does nothing to make her a better person or cause growth, it's just a part of her the new boyfriend might not like, and he might break up with her over it.)

▶ In order to get into the party, the protagonist will have to struggle against relying on a family that disowned her. (Yet using the family does nothing to change the protagonist, and she's not going to reconcile with them because of this.)

▶ In order to defeat the troll, the protagonist will have to struggle against what she considers an acceptable loss of life to prevent wide-scale death. (Yet possibly sacrificing a few lives to stop a rampaging troll isn't going to make her quit adventuring altogether.)

All the challenges offer internal struggles to resolve, but they're not about changing the life of the protagonist in a fundamental way.

Conflict and the Character Arc

Quite often, when writers talk about the internal conflict they actually mean the character arc and how the protagonist grows into a better person, but the two are *not* the same thing.

A character arc is how the character changes by undergoing the experiences of the novel. Since change comes from an internal struggle to make the right choice, the character arc uses the internal conflicts of the novel to cause that change. Often this change is positive and the character grows, but it can also be a negative change, turning a good or happy person into a bad or unhappy one. It could even be a change in perspective or belief, with a character ending the novel exactly where she started, just with a different worldview after her experiences.

The internal conflict shows the emotional struggle the character undergoes to change. The external challenges force the protagonist to face those internal struggles. What she decides to do affects who she is as a person and teaches her an important lesson—even if that lesson takes multiple attempts to sink in and effect change (which is part of the plot).

Angst over choosing the right course of action is not a character arc, though it does show internal conflict. Repeatedly making mistakes based on personal flaws or beliefs that keep you from being happy until you learn not to make those mistakes and change your ways is a character arc. And this takes both internal and external conflict to achieve.

For example:

▶ The protagonist who needs to abandon her criminal ways to be happy will face situations where she must choose to go the straight and narrow. Those choices will be hard, testing her resolve and giving her every opportunity to fail.

▶ The protagonist who needs to overcome her fear of rejection to find love will be put in situations where she can be rejected, so she can learn how to deal with them. Those situations will have consequences for failure, which will make it harder for her to overcome this problem.

▶ The protagonist who needs to gain the confidence to face her destiny and embrace who she truly is will find herself in situations that require confidence to succeed. She'll need to trust herself and have faith in her abilities to overcome her problems, and if she doesn't, she *will* fail.

The character arc uses the conflicts of the story to change the character.

However...

Some stories—such as thrillers or police procedurals, or novels in a series—don't have character arcs. While the protagonist usually faces internal conflicts, there's no change or growth from the beginning to the end of the story. Lee Child's Jack Reacher is a good example here. Reacher doesn't change, and there is rarely an internal conflict over what he has to do. He's presented with an external plot problem and he goes out and solves it. Many mysteries follow this same format— the novel is about solving the puzzle, not how the protagonist changes while solving that puzzle.

Some stories have small character arcs, where there's a little change, but it's not the reason for the novel. Readers are happy to see the protagonist learn and grow some, but they didn't pick up the book to see a character's emotional transformation. They just want to see her learn enough to not make the same mistakes over and over again.

Here are some reasons why a story might not need a character arc:

The story is more about the plot and less about the character: If the point of the story is to solve the plot problem, and the readers' enjoyment comes from the puzzle and the intellectual exercise of the plot, they don't usually care if the protagonist grows over the course of the novel. It's about the adventure, puzzle, or problem.

The hero of nearly every adventure story is in it for the adventure, not the emotional growth. The classic police detective of the police procedural genre typically solves the case and goes back to his life. The disaster movie shows how ordinary people deal with disaster. We love *Die Hard's* John McClane because defeats the bad guys by being a good cop. Sherlock Holmes captures our attention because he's brilliant and we want to see how he solves the mystery. We wanted to see the soldiers in Kelly's Heroes get to that Nazi gold and escape as rich men.

The protagonist is the moral or ethical center of the story: Some stories use the protagonist as the moral rock the world is trying to break. The story isn't about the protagonist changing, but their being the catalyst to change the world. The growth comes from everyone else in the novel, while the protagonist does not change.

My favorite example here is Marvel's *Captain America: The Winter Soldier.*

Steve "Captain America" Rogers has no character arc in this movie. He's the steady, rock-solid World War II hero he always has been, only now he's in the twenty-first century and dealing with the changing morals and ethics of a new world. His role in this story is to be the moral center, the reminder for everyone else who has lost their way of what it really means to be "the good guy."

Steve knows what's happening around him is wrong, and he does what he can to stop it and make his friends realize the dark path they're heading down. He saves the world by *not* changing and forcing others to live up to his example.

If your protagonist is the one who represents what's right, and everyone else is wrong, then they probably don't need to change. If the entire point of the story is to have the hero be the example everyone else finally comes around to, thereby narrowly avoiding "disaster" (however that happens in your story), it's their job to stand fast. They must face the ethical choices and take the hard path, even if it costs them a lot personally. They bring about the change.

The story is part of a series with stand-alone books: Certain series in certain genres have protagonists who never change—which is why readers love them. James Bond is always James Bond, and he never undergoes any deep, meaningful soul searching to learn a powerful lesson. The protagonist might become better at what they do over the course of the series, but they don't change who they are every book.

On some level, you could even argue many romances fit this category. They're two people falling in love. In some romances, those people need to change to find love, but in others, they're overcoming whatever external issue is keeping them apart. They fall in love despite the obstacles in their way because of who they are and that never changes.

If you're not sure if your story is one of these, ask if it would still make sense if you read the books out of order. If each book is its own story and there isn't a stronger multi-book plot for the entire series, odds are you don't need a character arc. But if each book builds on the previous one and the series doesn't really make sense unless read in the right order, there's a decent chance you do.

While character arcs are fantastic to show the depth of a character and explore an emotional theme, not every novel needs one. If you write in a heavily plot-centric genre, you might not have a character arc, even though you'll probably have internal conflicts. Don't feel you have to shove an arc into your novel if it doesn't work for your type of story.

Putting It All Together

The plot conflict is all about the external action—what the protagonist does to overcome the challenges. The character conflict is all about the internal struggle—why it's hard for the protagonist to make a decision and act. The character arc explores how the conflicts create a change in the character.

Thinking about conflict in terms of what the *challenge* is helps clarify the struggle, problem, or issue the protagonist is up against in each scene.

In essence, conflict is all about making your characters struggle to solve problems. A *lot*. And you have multiple options for how to do that.

Common Misconceptions about Conflict

Conflict is one of the more misunderstood aspects of writing fiction, because as we just saw, it's not always clear what someone means when they say, "conflict." This has no doubt tripped up a lot of new writers (and even some experienced writers), and caused quite a few unproductive writing sessions. It's hard to create strong conflict in a novel if you're not sure what conflict is.

If a writer learned only one aspect or believes a misconception (such as, all internal conflict is a character arc), it's quite likely she won't use, develop, or discover the right conflict needed for the story.

Here are some common misconceptions about conflict:

Misconception #1: Conflict = Fighting

It's not uncommon for writers to throw battles they don't need into a story, cause animosity between characters for no reason, and have characters behave antagonistically just to cause trouble—all because someone told them they "needed more conflict." To these writers, conflict is an actual fight—anything from an argument to a full-scale battle.

Not only does this limit available plot options, it creates a boring story, because nothing ever happens in the book but people fighting. Even worse, repeated fights seldom have conflict, because there's no struggle to do anything aside from "win." Take out the fights, and nothing really changes but the time it takes to get to the novel's climax.

For example:

▶ The fantasy protagonist who has to fight her way into the evil wizard's lair, past an ever-increasing number of henchmen. (The fights are all delays that don't change the outcome of the story. Get rid of half the fights and she still arrives at the correct moment the same as if she'd faced those fights.)

▶ The romance protagonist who has argument after argument with her mother about getting married. (The arguments cover the same information and nothing is ever resolved, but it feels like there's a lot of conflict because these two characters are always at odds.)

▶ The mystery protagonist who encounters uncalled-for hostility in every single person she questions—even if they're just random witnesses. (The hostility is there to make things appear tougher on the protagonist, but doesn't move the plot or affect the character at all.)

Conflict isn't always violent, nor should it be.

Misconception #2: Conflict = Tension

This has probably caused more frustration than any other aspect of conflict, because these two are so closely linked they seem like the same thing—except they *aren't*. You *can* have conflict without tension, and tension without conflict. Struggling over which boy to go to prom with *is* a conflict, but if there's no sense of anticipation about that choice, there's no tension. Sexual tension between characters keeps readers interested, even though there's no conflict since both parties want the same thing. The tension comes from the anticipation of how they resolve that attraction.

Tension is the reader's need to know what happens next, and the sense that there's more going on than meets the eye. It's the anticipation of something about to happen. That's it.

Conflict *creates* tension by putting a character into a situation where the outcome is uncertain, and readers anticipate what will happen or what will be discovered.

For example:

▶ The fantasy protagonist sneaks through the dark, scary grave-yard and jumps at every sound, sure she's being followed. (Being nervous isn't a conflict since there's nothing opposing the protagonist, but anticipating what might be following her can create tension in the reader.)

▶ The romance protagonist banters with the love interest, but never acts on her attraction and leaves without doing anything. (Playful bantering isn't a conflict, but readers eagerly read on to see where that banter might go, creating tension.)

▶ The mystery protagonist eavesdrops on a suspect. (The potential for being discovered isn't a conflict, but the fear that she might be found can create tension, as can the anticipation of what she might overhear.)

While all of these examples can be filled with tension, there's no opposition, no struggle, and no choice to be made to resolve any of them. Eagerly waiting for the next summer blockbuster to come out has tension, but no conflict. Trying to decide if you'll go see the movie on opening night, even though your best friend can't go with you and you promised to see it with her, is conflict.

Conflict works *with* tension (as well as stakes, and a slew of other things) to put characters into situations that make readers want to know what happens next, and thus read the novel you worked so hard on to find out.

Misconception #3: Conflict = What's "in the Way"

This is a tricky misconception, because technically, it's true—but it's also false. The obstacles in the way of the protagonist's goal are the challenges that need to be faced, and usually, there is conflict associated with overcoming or circumventing those obstacles. But sometimes, those obstacles are just things in the way.

For example:

▶ The fantasy protagonist must navigate the desolate wasteland to reach someone with answers she needs. (While the wasteland *could* contain conflicts, if nothing has changed for her between entering the wasteland and leaving the wasteland, she faced no conflicts.)

▶ The romance protagonists always have "something come up" to keep them from kissing or getting together. (While this might work once, or even twice if done with skill, the "near miss" is a contrived obstacle that doesn't create actual conflict.)

▶ The mystery protagonist speaks with multiple witnesses and no one has any information to move the plot along. (While speaking to people of interest is a critical part of a mystery, if nothing is ever gleaned, suggested, or learned from those conversations, they were only a delaying tactic and did nothing to create or affect the conflict.)

What's "in the way" should cause a challenge of some type or it isn't truly a conflict. If the result of resolving the challenge is the same as if the protagonist hadn't encountered the challenge in the first place, it's just an obstacle. Sometimes a scene just needs an obstacle, and that's okay, but if the conflict in most scenes is something in the way, that's a red flag the overall story lacks conflict.

Conflict encompasses such a wide range that it's easy to misunderstand and misuse. Just remember it's how both sides (external and internal) work together to challenge the protagonist and you'll avoid a lot of the common conflict pitfalls.

Why Writers Struggle with Conflict

With the various aspects and multiple misconceptions about conflict, it's easy to see why writers face difficulties when creating conflict in their novels. Over the years, I've pinpointed the three most common reasons writers stumble over conflict:

Reason #1: Conflict Isn't a "One-Size-Fits-All" Issue

What works for one story might not work for another, and even within the same novel, you'll have different aspects of conflict depending on the needs of the scene.

Conflict is the push and pull of the character as she experiences the story. It's the combination of the external with the internal that rounds out the conflict and gives meaning to what the protagonist does. These two sides work in tandem to illustrate why the problem of the novel (the core conflict) is worth reading about. What has to be done, why it's hard, and why it matters.

Something might technically be a conflict (two sides in opposition), but it doesn't make a good *story* conflict, because a strong story conflict has to also create a situation that drives a plot and leads readers through that story. For example, a shootout between outlaws holed up in a cabin, while the sheriff's posse tries to apprehend them, has plenty of conflict, but two sides shooting at each other for hours isn't a very interesting story.

If the situation doesn't do anything to create a strong story, it won't feel like an actual conflict. This is tough, because what constitutes a "strong story" can vary by person. Readers have biases, likes, and dislikes, and that contributes to how they regard story conflict.

For example:

▶ Romance readers who enjoy reading about two people overcoming emotional issues to fall in love might think a thriller with no emotional arc for the protagonist has no conflict, and is just a series of obstacles to overcome to solve some random problem.

▶ Thriller readers who want to see tough puzzles solved to prevent a catastrophe might think romances lack conflict because nothing ever really happens and the ending is obvious from the start.

▶ Science fiction readers who prefer novels that revolve around exploring ethical questions and the meaning of the universe might think fantasy novels that make up the rules of the world avoid actual conflict by making everything fit too perfectly.

And they're all right, and all wrong.

You can ask five people how strong your novel's conflict is, and it's possible to get five different answers ranging from weak to strong. Expectations affect how a reader might view your book. This is why it's important to get feedback from people who read your genre (or to read widely if you don't have beta readers). A strong story conflict to a mystery reader might not be the same as a strong conflict to a middle grade fantasy reader.

Reason #2: It's Not Always Clear What People Mean When They Say "Conflict"

Even beyond genre, conflict means different things to different people. If two writers are coming at it from two directions, there will very likely be misunderstandings about what they're actually talking about. Getting feedback such as, "your novel lacks conflict" isn't helpful if the person giving that feedback is referring to a *different* type of conflict.

For example, if you're thinking of the core conflict, you might assume:

- The conflict is the major problem the novel needs to resolve

- The conflict is connected to all the other problems in the novel in some way

- The conflict is the plot force driving the novel (and the protagonist)

But if another writer is referring to the *internal* conflict, they might think:

- The conflict is the emotional struggle the protagonist is facing

- The conflict will affect the protagonist's choices in the novel

- The conflict will cause the protagonist to reflect on the issues facing her and what they mean

One conflict is external and requires external actions; the other is internal and requires more reflection and thought. Neither is plotted or written the same way, and trying to plot the internal conflict the same as the external conflict will lead to some troublesome scenes. You might look at such a comment, point directly to the core conflict of your novel, and disregard the advice (and then pull your hair out when you keep getting rejected).

Context is everything, and if you don't understand which *type* of conflict someone is referring to, it can lead to a lot of frustration and confusion. You might think your novel has all the conflict it needs, so any "needs more conflict" feedback you get just flat out doesn't make sense to you.

For example:

Say you're looking at feedback from your latest critique. Some comments scattered throughout the manuscript include:

- There wasn't enough conflict

- I was never sure what the novel's conflict was

- The protagonist's conflict felt weak

Did the critiquer mean:

"There wasn't enough conflict" because there was a problem with the core conflict driving the novel, or the individual scene challenges? Or maybe there was a lack of stakes, making that critiquer not care about the conflict that was there? Did the critiquer really mean they wanted more tension? Maybe they thought every challenge was too quickly resolved?

"I was never sure what the novel's conflict was" because there wasn't a solid goal for the protagonist to solve? Or maybe there were too many goals or problems and nothing stood out as being the main issue? Was it a lack of motivation making what the protagonist wanted unclear?

"The protagonist's conflict felt weak" because every challenge was solved without effort? Or maybe there was nothing internal causing the protagonist to struggle with choices? Maybe it was because the climax didn't matter to anyone in any significant way?

Unless the critiquer is clear about what the issue is, the writer might assume the wrong thing about the actual weakness of the story.

For example:

Let's say the writer believes in misconception #3 and thinks conflict is an obstacle in the way of the protagonist's goal. If so, then she might think:

"There wasn't enough conflict" means the critiquer felt the writer should put more obstacles in the way, and have more "stuff" that the protagonist must do to resolve a goal. But adding "stuff" only compounds the problem by adding tasks that have no meaning and do nothing to affect the story. No new information or insight is revealed by completing that task or overcoming that challenge—and often, no challenge is involved in completing this task. Climbing a ladder with ten rungs is no different from climbing a ladder with five rungs if it takes no extra effort to get to the top of the ladder.

"I was never sure what the novel's conflict was" means the critiquer felt the climax wasn't clear and exactly what the protagonist had to do wasn't obvious, so the writer needs to tell the reader exactly what was going on and what it all means. But this only leads to a climax that feels told and explanatory, and does nothing to fix the actual problem if the critiquer understood the challenge the protagonist faced, but thought it was too easy to resolve and didn't offer the protagonist an emotional challenge.

"The protagonist's conflict felt weak" means the critiquer felt the specific obstacles the protagonist faced in each scene weren't hard enough, so the writer goes over the top to create melodramatic challenges with multiple steps to overcome each obstacle. "Weak" is perceived as "needs to be more complicated," not "needs to be more emotionally difficult to decide what to do." Just making the obstacle harder or more complicated doesn't address the lack of *motivations* for the protagonist to face those challenges in the first place. The conflict was "weak" because there was no reason to face the challenge, not because the challenge was too easy.

Assuming the wrong type of conflict, or misunderstanding what the word "conflict" means to the critiquer, can cause a writer to change what doesn't need fixing and ignore what does. This can lead to a novel that keeps getting the same feedback, even though the writer feels she's addressed those concerns over and over again. And *that* can lead to a very frustrated and unhappy writer. When in doubt, *ask* your critiquer to clarify.

Special note for critiquers: All of this is just as important when critiquing someone's work as it is when getting critiqued. Remember to be as clear as possible what you mean and specify where something in a manuscript is lacking (or excelling). The clearer you are about any conflict issues, the easier it will be for the writer to address those issues.

Reason #3: Using the Wrong Conflict Makes It Harder to Write the Novel

Use the wrong conflict and things don't quite mesh in a novel. This is most often seen when trying to plot using the internal conflict of the character arc. For example, an internal conflict might work wonderfully to support the character arc, but internal conflicts don't create plot—

they just make it emotionally *harder* to overcome those external challenges. What the character physically does to resolve that internal conflict is the plot.

Let's explore this further using one of the examples:

Say you have a novel about a woman with a criminal past who gets out of prison and wants to go the straight and narrow and get her life back together. That's a character arc—to get what she needs (her life back together) she has to change her ways. Many writers would say this book is about "a woman who gets her life back together after she's released from prison." And they're right—but many of those same writers would have trouble creating a plot to support this story.

The reason? There's no conflict in that description of the book.

"Getting her life back together" doesn't show a plot, because nothing in this statement provides an external goal to pursue. There's also no conflict—nothing is preventing her from getting her life back together. Without those details, the goal isn't specific enough to know what external challenges she might face as she tries to get her life back together.

However, "getting her life back together" *is* a solid character arc to explore. It's what she *does* to put her life back together that will create the plot, and what's preventing her from putting her life back together will create the conflicts (both internal and external).

Without knowing the details of those two things, you can't write this book. If you try, you'll most likely end up with fifty to one hundred pages that show the protagonist getting out of jail, returning to normal life, and interacting with the people she left behind, plus a lot of backstory that explains how she ended up in prison in the first place and why she wants to change.

And then it'll probably stall, because there's no conflict to drive the plot forward and give the protagonist something to do once the setup is over. If you're reading this book, odds are this has happened to you at least once. If you have a manuscript that's stalled before page one hundred, it might be a good idea to examine your conflict to make sure there's a conflict or challenge for your protagonist to face and overcome to move the plot forward.

Trying to plot with a character arc can create a lot of frustration for writers, because the focus is on the internal struggle to change, not the external action, so the specific tasks (the goals) aren't as defined as they need to be. It's like trying to bake a cake without putting it into the oven. The external heat is what turns the ingredients into dessert.

To figure out what those two details are and find the conflicts of this story we'd ask:

1. What constitutes "getting her life back together"

2. What's preventing her from doing that?

Let's say she wants to return to school to be a counselor so she'll be able to use her own mistakes to help others avoid her fate. Maybe she met a counselor in prison who made a difference for her, and she wants to follow in her footsteps. Her goal: return to school and get her degree.

Now the book is about a woman who wants to go back to school after her release from prison. But notice there's still no conflict. She has a solid goal, and we can see how this plot is likely to unfold (how she goes back to school), but we need to be more specific about what challenges she might encounter in pursuit of this goal.

What are some possible conflicts she could face in trying to return to school? The first problems that pop into my head are:

- Money to pay tuition and support herself

- Admission to the school she wants

- Past associates who want her to go back to crime

These are potential obstacles she might face, but they're still not conflicts, because there's nothing preventing her from doing these things yet. Let's choose the money issue as her goal, because money and crime have the strongest potential for conflict. Let's also play with past associates who might lure her back to her old life. These cover both external and internal conflicts. How might we turn these obstacles into tough challenges?

She'll need money to pay tuition, so that means a job that pays enough to cover all her bills and school, financial aid, or a scholarship. This is the honest, non-criminal way to achieve her goal of going to school.

But maybe no one will hire an ex-con, or she can only get part-time jobs that pay under minimum wage. If she can't get a decent job, she can't support herself, and she can't pay for school. Without a job and with her criminal record, she's a bad risk and no bank will give her financial aid. She barely graduated from high school, so she's not eligible for any scholarships. Getting the cash for school is no longer easy.

But it's still *possible* if she's willing to work multiple jobs and take one class a semester. It'll take her longer, but if she's patient, she'll get there (and be a pretty boring book).

That's where the past associates come in. They're a tempting carrot to create a little internal conflict to draw her back into the life she wants to leave behind.

What if these associates ask her to help rob a rich guy rumored to keep a lot of cash around the house? It goes against her need to go legit, but *does* fulfill her desire to pay for tuition. Her internal conflict is between taking the easy path of crime to get what she wants, or the harder path of legality to get what she wants.

Now there's conflict that challenges both her external need to pay for tuition, and her internal need to not steal anymore. She can't have both, so which does she choose?

Since she wants to stay away from crime, of course she says no—it's common to show the protagonist trying and failing at the start of the character arc. She does her best, but her job search won't go well, and any job she does get will not last. Her past will haunt her and create more trouble for her, keeping her from her goal of school and her need to get her life in order.

But the harder it gets to be good, the easier it is to decide she can handle "one more job" and get out. Which of course goes badly, gets her into more trouble, and pushes her even farther from her goals. It won't be until she accepts the harder path that things will start to turn her way—but only if she works for it and grows as a person.

At its most basic, conflict (internal or external) is the challenge to overcome whatever is preventing the protagonist from doing what needs to be done—physically, emotionally, or mentally—to resolve a problem and move forward.

To truly understand conflict and how to use it, we need to first understand the other writing elements that affect it.

Things That Affect Conflict

Since conflict is deeply connected to so many aspects of a novel, it's impossible to talk about it without understanding what affects it and what helps create that conflict. This is why it's easy to mistake one type for another, and get confused about what people mean when they refer to conflict. For example, readers "not caring about what happens" could indicate a lack of stakes, while claiming "nothing happens" could be due to a lack of goals or motivations, or a general sense of *"meh"* could be the result of low to missing tension—but each reader might say, "There's no conflict," because the issue is in how those aspects *affect* the conflict, not the conflict itself.

In this section I've used real-world examples from movies and TV shows to further examine the topics discussed. If you haven't seen these movies or shows and feel the examples might confuse you more than help you, it's okay to skip them. They're optional for those who want to dig a little deeper, or who want an example they can study on their own time at their leisure.

Let's dive in.

The Genre: What Readers Expect from the Conflict

Your novel's genre influences what types of conflicts will be at the core of that novel, and what types of conflicts the reader expects. This can drive you crazy when you're trying to figure out how to use conflict in your writing.

For example:

- If everyone keeps telling you, "all novels need a strong character arc," you might think you need to shove an emotional journey subplot into your police procedural (when what you have is just fine for that genre).

- If you heed advice from thriller writers, you might force an action-packed plot into your literary novel (which ruins your quiet character journey about redemption).

In essence, the genre determines what challenges the protagonist will struggle with over the course of the novel. Thrillers explore how the protagonist struggles to outsmart a worthy foe and make hard choices about people's lives. Mysteries revolve around the struggle to be smarter than the criminal—focusing on the procedures and challenges required to solve a crime or puzzle. Literary novels show the character's journey and the emotional struggles that change the protagonist, while romances explore the reasons two people are kept apart and the challenges they face to be together.

Different genres have different expectations, and readers typically want to see a certain type of conflict central to those genres.

For example:

- A happily-ever-after romance isn't likely to have a core conflict that revolves around stopping a madman from blowing up the town hall.

- A thriller probably won't have a core conflict that revolves around the two main characters overcoming their personal hangups and falling in love.

- A literary novel usually doesn't have a core conflict that revolves around stopping a serial killer.

One caveat here: With novels that mix genres, there is wiggle room for the type of conflict. For example, romantic suspense readers expect a thrill mixed in with their courtship dance. Almost every novel regardless of genre has some type of "mystery" to solve. When you mix genres, each genre's conflict expectations will also potentially affect the novel.

While all novels have both internal and external conflicts, the genre also influences how *strong* they will be in that novel. Plot-driven novels typically have conflicts that are more external and plot based, so the challenges frequently revolve around external issues. Character-driven novels typically explore internal conflicts that lead to character growth, so the challenges will be over internal issues and support a character arc more. Plenty of novels have both, using the external conflicts to bring about the internal growth of the characters, so the challenges will be over external factors that *cause* that internal struggle.

Keep in mind what type of conflicts are common in your genre and how they challenge your protagonist.

The Antagonist: The Person or Thing Driving the Conflict

Since so many stories are about one person trying to prevent another person from acting, the antagonist is the embodiment of the conflict. The villain, the bad guy, the one trying to muck up the entire plan and create chaos. We can't talk about conflict without asking, "Who's the antagonist?"

Because we so closely associate the antagonist with a person, it's easy to forget that the real question is, "Who *or what* is the antagonist?" It's not always a person, even if a person represents the conflict of the story.

For example:

▶ In *The Lottery*, the antagonist is the society that stones people to death (Person vs. Society).

▶ In *Jaws*, the antagonist is a shark (Person vs. Nature).

▶ In *The Matrix*, the antagonist is the technology enslaving mankind (Person vs. Society/Technology).

The people in these stories are affected by the antagonist, such as the mayor in *Jaws* effectively "siding" with the shark to keep the beaches open, opposing Sheriff Brody's goal of closing the beaches to protect the people. The conflict is, "shark wants to be a shark," and that causes trouble for Brody and the town—but the *people* were actively opposing Brody's desire to close the beaches. The conflict came from the choice of, "Do I risk my job by opposing the mayor and closing the beaches, thus losing the town millions in revenue, or do I protect visitors from possibly being eaten by a shark?" An external conflict with an internal struggle.

The shark created the challenge Brody had to face, and the conflict had ripple effects throughout the story (as good conflicts do). How the other characters in the story dealt with that conflict put Brody in tougher and tougher situations and forced him to make harder and harder choices.

In essence, the antagonist is the person or thing responsible for the challenges in the first place. What the other characters do about that creates the conflict (and plot) of the novel.

What *Mama* Can Teach Us about Antagonists

Once in a while, a story comes along that blows me away. It might be a novel, a movie, a game, or a TV show, but how it's written or structured illustrates an aspect of storytelling that expands my writer's mind.

The film, *Mama*, by Andrés and Barbara Muschietti is one such story. How it handles antagonists is a thing of beauty we can all learn from.

The premise is this: Two young girls abandoned in the woods are rescued by a tormented spirit who decides to raise them as her own. When the girls are found five years later, things get...complicated.

Although classified as horror, this film is more psychological suspense in the "peek-through- your-fingers-while-on-the-edge-of-your-seat" way. It will utterly creep you out, but also make you laugh so hard you can't breathe. And it makes you care—deeply—due to the incredible conflicts it creates among these characters.

There's no true "bad guy" in this film. Everyone has an agenda, but each character also has the best interests of the children at heart. They're all antagonists to Mama's goal of keeping the children, even though she's technically the antagonist of the film.

Here's what's so good about *Mama*:

It provides an antagonist you sympathize with, even though everything says you probably shouldn't.

Mama is a tortured spirit, but she saves small children (one and three years old) and cares for them when they would have otherwise died. But she also has a homicidal side that's not especially kid-friendly. We know all this, we see how deadly she can be, but we still wish they could all just live happily ever after. We *care* about Mama's goal, even when she's freaking us out by her creepiness.

How this affects the conflict: Antagonists with relatable goals can make readers care more deeply about what's going on in the story. The antagonist whose goal makes sense makes the conflict that much more interesting for readers, because they see both sides of it.

It offers incredibly well-rounded conflict not based on good vs. evil.

This is where so much of the genius of the film springs from. The conflicts are real, human, and based on complex (yet simple) emotions. Who *can't* understand the love and devotion of a mother for her children? Who can't understand the loyalty those children would feel for their mother? But that becomes something much more complicated when you add in the spirit aspect and an uncle who also loves his nieces and wants them to be safe and happy. And then there's his girlfriend, who never wanted to be a mom, but is now struggling with two extremely weird and damaged kids. Even the psychologist who wants to take them away for their own good has the children's best interests at heart. Every character has a conflict that's both relatable and understandable, but no one is "evil." Not even Mama.

How this affects the conflict: Sometimes the best conflicts come from people trying to help, not hurt. "What's preventing the protagonist from getting what she wants" can be helpful as easily as hurtful. A situation with no right answer can be a fertile field for conflict.

It has layered characters who feel like real people.

Every character in this movie could have easily turned into a cliché, but they didn't, because they were real and layered people. The girlfriend is a perfect example. Her boyfriend (the girls' uncle) has been searching for his nieces for five years, and she fully supports that even as he's going broke. Many stories would have made this a source of conflict between them with arguing and antagonism.

When the uncle finds the girls, and they're feral, she sticks by him and keeps supporting him. It's clear this isn't what she signed up for, but it's the right thing to do because she loves him, and these girls need help and support. This character could have become the whiny, bitchy girlfriend, but instead she became a rich person struggling to do the right thing under extraordinary circumstances.

How this affects the conflict: You can develop well-crafted conflicts by creating real people with layered, complex emotions and desires and giving them a challenge to overcome. One-dimensional characters will act one dimensionally, and thus become predictable. But rich, layered characters bring more options and interest to the story.

You never know what to expect, because it defies expectations.

Unpredictability is often difficult because there are only so many logical things that can happen in a scene. With *Mama*, you're never sure where the story is going to go, because Mama has such a strong and compelling story arc herself. She *could* win, because you care about what happens to her. Her conflict, even though she is technically the "bad guy," is compelling, and part of you *wants* her to keep the children.

It plays off viewer expectations in a masterful way. You think "evil spirit," but Mama defies that by her love for these children. She acts in ways you don't expect spirits to act, and the children she's saved treat her as Mama, and not an evil spirit. Those relationships change everything.

Mix in the varied emotions, and you're laughing at things that are scary, gasping at things that are sweet, and crawling out of your skin when things are completely normal. It turns what you know and how you feel upside down.

How this affects the conflict: Look for the unexpected in your conflicts and don't fall back on clichés or stereotypes, or even classic tropes. The more you surprise your readers, the more you draw them into the story because they'll be dying to know what happens next.

It has masterful pacing and manipulation of tension.

By the end of the movie, you feel as if you've run a marathon. It puts you through the emotional wringer, but you enjoy every nervous step, because you never know what the payoff will be. Sometimes it's a scare, but just as often it's something funny or flat out adorable.

Scenes creep by when you need to feel every step, but they rush when the intent is to make you gasp. And sometimes, one comes immediately after the other, so before long, the slower scenes are almost more tense than the ones that take your breath away. You *know* something's about to happen and have no idea what it will be or how it will make you feel.

How this affects the conflict: Every scene is created to evoke emotion from viewers and make them care about the outcome of these conflicts. The writers and director vary that emotion in a wonderful rise and fall of feelings and anticipation that draws you in and holds you there. You care, so you're invested in how these conflicts turn out.

It provides an ending that's perfect for the story, even if it's not the ending viewers probably wanted.

With a story like *Mama*, happily ever after would have felt wrong, but so would something dark and depressing. Because you want so many different things for these characters by the end of the film, it's hard to know what a "win" would be. The writers handled it perfectly. You want to cry (and might, I did a little), but you know in your heart that it *had* to go that way.

It might not end the way you want it to, but that's okay. It has the right ending for the story arcs presented. It's a rare story that can *not* give viewers/readers what they want and still satisfy them.

How this affects the conflict: What's right for the characters can also be right for the readers if you set it up correctly. A strong resolution to a well-crafted story arc can be much more satisfying an ending than a "right" or "happy" ending if there's no basis for it.

Mama proves that antagonists don't have to be evil or cause problems to create a successful conflict. Even when every character in the story wants the same thing, conflict can develop through not knowing what the right thing to do *is*. Antagonist doesn't mean villain, and not every "bad guy" is all bad.

The Goals and Motivations: The Reasons for the Conflict

The protagonist's goal is the reason a conflict exists in the first place—she wants it, and someone or something is keeping her from it (that opposing force). The protagonist's motivation for that goal (why she wants it) is what makes readers care about the outcome.

This is the basis for the classic GMC (Goals-Motivation-Conflict) trinity of storytelling. The goal is created by the motivation (what the protagonist wants and why), which *leads* to the conflict (what's preventing the protagonist from getting it). A lack of GMC is why random conflict feels contrived and uninteresting.

For example (and bear with me, because this is going to get a little silly):

Evil wizard: **"Haha! I shall enslave this town and force everyone to work** in the mines."

Protagonist: "Okay." Then she moves away.

If the protagonist has no desire or need to stop the antagonist, she won't try. If she won't try, there is nothing in conflict. Forcing her to stay and fight feels shallow without a solid reason behind that decision.

Evil wizard: "Haha! I shall enslave this town and force everyone to work in the mines."

Protagonist: "No you won't, I shall stop you."

Evil wizard: "Why?"

Protagonist: "Uh, 'cause slavery is bad?"

Now our protagonist has a goal, but her reason for risking her life is weak (aside from the fact that it's always a good idea to stop evil wizards from enslaving lands). There's a conflict, but with nothing behind the goal but some lip service, the protagonist can pack up and leave as soon as things get rough. She has no solid motivation to take on the evil wizard. So let's *give* her a reason.

Evil wizard: "Haha! I shall enslave this town and force everyone to work in the mines."

Protagonist: "No you won't, I shall stop you."

Evil wizard: "Why?"

Protagonist: "My family has lived in this town for generations! I know these people and care about their lives, and I will defend them to my last breath. I shall not see those lives ripped from them for your petty gain."

Evil wizard: "Yeah, okay, this sounds like too much work. I'll try the town next door."

Wait…what? See, goals and motivations *aren't* just for the good guys. Without a strong motivation to act, even the bad guys can walk away from the conflict when things get tough. And if they don't, readers might wonder why this guy is fighting so hard for absolutely no reason. Even if the conflict involves two sides fighting over a town filled with people, neither side actually cares or has any reason to fight. Let's give our bad guy his own motives and see what happens.

Evil wizard: "Haha! I shall enslave this town and force everyone to work in the mines, because a bigger, eviler wizard is trying to steal my territory and I need resources to fight him off."

Protagonist: "No you won't! I shall stop you to save the people that I love and preserve their way of life."

Evil wizard: "Then we shall fight to the last soul!"

Townsfolk: "Excuse me? We'll be happy to work the mines for a fair wage if that means keeping that other evil dude off our doorstep."

Evil wizard: "You will? Because that would seriously free up my minions to fend off the other wizard instead of standing guard over you guys."

Protagonist: "But he's an evil wizard!"

Townsfolk: "Have you *seen* the job market out there? This will be a *huge* boost to our local economy."

And now we see why "life and death" stakes don't always work to create a strong conflict. If the problem can be easily resolved, there's still no conflict. Unless the evil wizard is determined to cause pain and suffering (and he'd need a good reason to do so, otherwise his actions will feel contrived), a non-violent way to resolve his problem is a far more likely approach.

Regardless of genre, we see this type of conflict all the time in fiction. One side is acting to be "evil" and the other side is fighting against it. But when we dig down a little and ask why, there's no good answer. Evil is being evil for evil's sake, and good is being good for good's sake. The conflict is manufactured and based on superficial elements.

One caveat here: There *are* stories, such as fairy tales and horror, where evil *is* just evil. The difference is in the antagonist. Monsters can be evil because they aren't people. Just like in *Jaws*, a shark eating people is just being a shark. It doesn't need motivation, though "I'm hungry" *is* a perfectly acceptable reason for eating people from the shark's perspective. But *people* being monstrous typically need reasons or their actions feel shallow at best, contrived at worst.

This holds true for the thriller (crazed madman wants to blow up a landmark because he's crazy), the mystery (killer murders lots of people in complicated ways just because), the romance (couple fight and don't like each other because of a misunderstanding that would be resolved in two minutes if they spoke to each other about it), the fantasy (antagonist decides to summon demons to destroy the world, just so the hero has a reason to do something), or any other novel that relies on someone being bad and someone being good and both characters trying to stop each other without cause.

Strong conflicts come from strong goals and stronger motivations. Let's see what happens with our town when we toss in some personal issues behind the protagonist's motivation.

Evil wizard: "Haha! I shall offer this town a decent wage to mine the resources I need, because a bigger, eviler wizard is trying to steal my territory and I need help fighting him off. In return, I will protect this town as long as it's beneficial to me."

Protagonist: "No you won't! I shall not allow you to take advantage of these people!"

Townsfolk: "Sounds like a good deal to me."

Protagonist: "But I'm your hero! It's my job to protect you from evil. That's why you love me, and I need that validation or my life is meaningless. I have nothing else."

Townsfolk: "Your personal hangups are not our concern. We told you to learn a real skill, not all that sword swinging and inspirational speaking. This deal protects the town better than one gal with a shiny stick."

Evil wizard: "We have an agreement then?"

Townsfolk: "We do. I'll send you a contract by the end of the day."

Protagonist (muttering): "I'll show them! I'll sabotage their efforts so they're open to attack, and then fight off that other, *eviler* wizard to prove that I am *indeed* the hero this town deserves, and then they will love me again!"

Evil wizard: "Is this gal for real?"

Townsfolk (sighing): "Afraid so. We keep trying to get her help, but her parents were killed by an evil wizard and now she won't stop putting herself in harm's way."

Evil wizard: "Her interference is seriously going to complicate things."

Townsfolk: "I know. We'll deal with that when we have to. Her parents died saving the town, so we kinda owe them."

As ridiculous as this example has gotten, aren't you much more interested in how this last problem turns out? We have a town struggling to survive not only an attack from an evil wizard, but job loss and economic hardship. We have a wizard struggling to protect his own territory, who might lose it because some would-be hero with emotional baggage will get in the way of his plans. We have a local gal struggling to live up to her parents' memory, who doesn't realize she's her own worst enemy here and is creating the reasons why no one in the town loves her.

In other words, we have conflict backed by goals and motivations.

If the only reason the protagonist wants to oppose the antagonist (and vice versa) is because she's the good guy and he's the bad guy, then you're missing an opportunity to create real conflict by adding a strong goal and a personal motivation to strive for that goal and cause that conflict.

Let's look next at a real-world example.

Optional: What *Scandal* Can Teach Us about Goals and Motivations

The first season of the TV show *Scandal* has some of the best plotting and tension I've ever seen, because it has a firm hold on its characters' goals and motivations. *All* the characters have strong goals backed by solid motivations, so you always feel that anything can happen at any moment and you're dying to know what happens next.

It's just seven episodes, so it unfolds more like a long movie than a series. This makes it easy to watch and study how the writers and creators of this show handled the many conflicts the characters struggle with.

Scandal centers around Olivia Pope (Kerry Washington), a political fixer who ran the president's election campaign and is now helping others fix their problems (usually scandals, hence the name). She and her staff call themselves Gladiators, and typically fight for "the good guys," or at least help those who haven't done what they're being accused of. But in the political realm of Washington, DC, it's often hard to know who the good guys actually are (which is a good example of how an environment full of inherent conflict can be used to strengthen a story).

The first season's main story arc is worthy of any great political mystery or thriller. It focuses on a woman claiming to be the president's mistress, and the White House coming to Olivia to help fix the ensuing scandal. This is tough for Olivia because A) she doesn't want to work for the White House anymore and B) she had an affair with President Grant during the campaign and they are the loves of each others' lives. She doesn't believe he had the affair and takes the case to prove that. This is a great example of how the internal conflict can affect the external goals. Working with the president tempts her to rekindle the affair, which is what she's trying to protect him from.

It's not long before the story twists and turns and dives. You never know where it's going or what's going to happen next and you're glued to the screen to find out. The tension is fabulous and the pacing fantastic. You *need* to find out what's *really* going on—and that's the beauty of the multiple layers of conflict in this show. Everyone faces challenges and struggles to choose the right way to handle those challenges, but there is no "right way" that's good for all involved. This is the element worth capturing in your own novel.

Here are a few of the things *Scandal* does so well to create conflict through goals and motivations:

Everyone has secrets.

Every character has a past and things to hide, so they're personally motivated to protect these secrets, even at the expense of the story goal. Some secrets are small, more embarrassing than dangerous, while others could bring down regimes.

How this affects the conflict: Characters with things to hide will act in ways to keep those secrets hidden. These characters can be obstacles to your protagonist's goal without actually being villains, because it's not about the protagonist—it's about keeping *their* secret. Sure, the best friend *wants* to help the hero save his mother, but that requires revealing that he spent six years working as muscle for the local drug dealer. He'd be ruined if anyone found out, so he doesn't share his contacts or admit that he recognizes the man in the photo connected to Mom's kidnapping.

Secrets don't need to be this dangerous to be effective, though. Avoiding things that skirt too close to something embarrassing can also cause trouble if it distracts the protagonist and works as a red herring. Why is Jane lying? Is she in on the evil plan? What is she avoiding?

Viewers (readers) don't know what they *think* they know.

This is my favorite aspect of the show. You think you know the truth about a character or a situation, and as you uncover delicious facts and details and you're sure you have it all figured out—*wham!* You get one more piece of the puzzle and everything you thought you knew has changed—because you never knew the *true* goal or why someone wanted it. A character you were sure was a victim turns out to be the villain. A fact you knew was true turns out to be a lie. Characters you'd never trust turn out to be the people who can save the day.

How this affects the conflict: A character's goal and motivations can be used to trick readers, lie to them, and lead them down the wrong path (in a good way). Hiding the *real* goal can help create conflict in the story, because odds are the protagonist won't know that real goal either. She'll act based on what she thinks is true when someone is hiding things from her. A character with a secret motive might also try to prevent the protagonist from acting, and those reasons could be misunderstood in delicious conflict-creating ways. Just don't tip it *too* far—it can become a problem if the author purposefully hides information a character would have known or figured out *just* to trick readers or force a conflict that wouldn't naturally occur.

The characters lie.

Olivia Pope has her team of investigators verify *everything* they learn, because they know that no one—especially powerful people in trouble—tells the whole truth. People lie, even if it's not malicious in nature. These lies cause trouble (conflicts) because if Olivia doesn't have the whole picture, she can't help her clients. When she doesn't understand the real goals and motivations behind the choices and decisions, she acts on bad information—which leads to wonderful disasters.

How this affects the conflict: Lies can delay actions or revelations, influence decisions and behaviors, or change the path the protagonist takes (leading directly to more conflict). White lies told to spare some-one's feelings could turn out to be horrible mistakes that cause tremen-dous trouble. Unraveling lies could be the challenge to solving a prob-lem. Not every character has to be a liar (that would get tedious), but people usually don't volunteer exactly the information someone needs when they need it, and their reasons for it vary wildly.

Characters work at cross purposes.

Olivia frequently clashes with Cyrus Beene, the White House Chief of Staff. They both want to help the president, but she does what *she* thinks is best, and *he* does what he thinks is best (classic conflict situation). These plans often flat out contradict each other. Even when they're both trying to accomplish the same task, they can make things worse by not talking to each other first.

How this affects the conflict: Characters can be wrapped up in their own lives and problems and just not think to tell anyone what they're doing. They might have the same end goal in mind, but have different ideas on how to get there and act without sharing that information with other characters. Sidekicks might try to help and inadvertently change how the plot unfolds. Actions by other characters might affect the plans of the protagonist. Good intentions can turn into the very obstacle pre-venting the protagonist from acting or succeeding.

Answers lead to more questions.

Scandal's pacing of reveals is beautifully done. You get an answer, and it's great, but it leads to more questions and you're eager for the next piece of the puzzle. Every bit of information is rationed out so there's always something you *need* to know. *Scandal* also mixes up the size of the reveals, so sometimes they're small details you were curious about, and other times they're major plot-changing twists.

How this affects the conflict: Readers might notice a character has an agenda (a goal) that's not in the protagonist's best interests. They'll be intrigued and want to know why. They might wonder why one charac-ter is trying so hard to avoid another character—and wonder what hap-pened between them. Readers might wonder if a character is telling the truth or not—and wonder if that character is really on the protagonist's side. It's all about tiny breadcrumbs leading the reader to the payoff. But be careful—if you give too much away too fast, there's nothing for readers to crave.

Season one of *Scandal* is a fun and educational way to see how to weave goals and motivations into your story to create strong conflicts that keep readers hooked.

The Stakes: The Reason the Conflict Matters

Stakes are the consequences facing the protagonist if she fails to overcome her challenges. They're the "or else" in a threat, the "I didn't see that coming" in a plan, and the "worst that can happen" in a risk. The more the consequences affect the protagonist personally, the higher the stakes will feel to readers. In most cases, the more personal the stakes, the stronger the conflict, because there's more to lose.

Without stakes, the conflict is just "something in the way."

Stakes are often misunderstood, especially since people like me advise you to make them as high as possible (which is good advice, but "high stakes" isn't what everyone thinks it is). High stakes aren't stakes in which the world is ending and there's a total disaster on the way. They have nothing to do with the size of the consequence or the number of people who might suffer from it. High stakes are stakes that affect the protagonist in a profound and meaningful way that matters to readers.

For example:

- Big, end-of-the-world stakes are exciting and huge and wonderful, but they happen to *everyone* in that world, not just the protagonist, so why care about one person over millions?

- Small, my-life-is-going-to-change stakes are personal and wonderful, and they often happen just to the protagonist, so it's easier to relate to the risk and care about the character and her problem.

From a purely structural standpoint, personal goals + personal stakes = personal action, and that's what plot is all about: the individual conflicts that illustrate the protagonist's struggle to win. If the risk is personal, the character's motivations are much clearer and it's easier to determine what she'll do and why, because the stakes will be clearer, too.

Let's look at a typical high-stakes story idea: A man learns an asteroid will hit Earth in six months and prepares himself for the end of the world.

Is there a conflict here?

Some will say yes, others no. I would say no, because there's nothing the man can do about the problem, and there's nothing here that shows why "preparing himself" is going to be difficult (aside from the obvious "we're all going to die" thing). So while it seems like the highest stakes of all, there's really no conflict. Nothing about this setup shows anything keeping the man from preparing.

What about this: A terminally ill man learns he has six months to live and sets out to find the son he abandoned.

Is there a conflict here?

I still say no-ish, because there's also nothing here that shows how this is going to be difficult. This is what he has to do, but what's preventing him from doing it?

However, an abandoned son has *inherent* conflict of its own, so we can guess where *potential* conflict might lie, even though that's not clearly stated—which is where trouble can lie with conflict if you're not clear about it. Not everyone will assume the same thing you do, and what's worse, if you're not clear about the conflict in your mind, you might not make it clear in the novel. Sure, we can assume just finding the son could be a challenge if the father doesn't have access to more than Google. Plus, odds are the son isn't going to welcome his father with open arms and forgive him for taking off. But none of this is *stated* in the story description, so we can't be sure the writer plans to do any of those things. The writer might not even know at this point (which is why some novels hit a wall in the first fifty pages).

But what if we clarify that goal for the father in how we *state* our conflict?

A terminally ill man learns he has six months to live and sets out to reconcile with the son he abandoned.

One word change, but "reconcile" is a clear goal with conflict, and it's much harder than simply "finding" the son with a vague assumption that also means reconciling. Now we see the *specific* goal the conflict will come from—he wants to fix his relationship with his son before he dies and the son probably won't want that. How resistant to reconciliation the son is will determine how strong this conflict is, and how much the father will have to struggle to resolve it.

Not every story is going to require deep, soul-wrenching, personal stakes, but it doesn't hurt to consider what the protagonist is risking versus the average person. Even in an action-focused thriller with lots of people at risk, there's usually one character who has more to lose than anyone else.

Stakes make readers care about the conflict in the scene. The more compelling your stakes, the more compelled readers will be to see how your protagonist will resolve the conflict she's facing.

Let's examine a story that *should* have worked, but didn't, due to a lack of stakes.

Optional: What *Burnt* Can Teach Us about Stakes

The movie *Burnt* is technically well done. It has an amazing cast, great actors and acting, good production values, strong writing, solid bones in the plot—everything a good story ought to have to be successful. What it lacks are *stakes*.

In *Burnt*, Adam Jones (Bradley Cooper) is a chef who destroyed his career with drugs and diva behavior. He sobers up and returns to London to redeem himself by opening up a top restaurant and gaining three Michelin stars. Classic redemption story of the Person vs. Self conflict type, with a strong potential character arc to boot—can he change his ways enough to be successful and get his stars, or will he crash and burn again?

Adam has all the makings of a wonderful character with past problems hurting his future—a talented chef with a rough past who threw it all away and is desperate to regain what he lost. He burned bridges and ruined relationships, and pretty much did everything he could to ensure he'd never work as a chef again. The struggle for redemption is right there, rife with a ton of inherent conflict.

Except...

None of his troubled past matters. Nothing he once did has any ramifications on what he wants to do now. There's no antagonist. No one is standing in his way of getting his stars. The only obstacle he faces is that he has to randomly wait for the Michelin people to show up and judge him.

The *potential* for high-stakes conflict is there:

- The sous chef he wants to hire doesn't want to work for him.

- He needs a past colleague he betrayed to work with him again.

- He has no money to start his restaurant and his reputation makes him a bad risk.

- He must deal with the personal failings as a human being that ruined him the first time.

Great problems to overcome, right? But *nothing* is actually a problem. These are all just tasks he completes with little to no effort.

- He speaks to the restaurant owners and the sous chef gets fired so she can work for him. And she does. And stays, even though he treats her like dirt—but getting her fired *could* have been a strong source of additional conflict, or a challenge that took effort and personal change on his part to achieve.

- The colleague comes to work for him when he asks, with "no hard feelings" about the betrayal (more on this later).

- His old boss vouches for him, and as long as Adam takes a drug test every week and goes to a therapist, the old boss will financially back the restaurant. There's a hint of stakes here, but there's no conflict to Adam getting the money. He asks, he receives.

- Adam's being a horrible human being is overlooked by everyone because "he's so talented" so the thing that caused his downfall isn't a problem anymore, and he doesn't have to grow to succeed.

What Adam wants, Adam gets, no problems whatsoever. He doesn't have to struggle to overcome anything at all. His "flaws" don't hurt him even though they should. He's actually *admired* for being a royal jerk and treating everyone around him badly.

There's a hint of potential conflict at the end of act two when the Michelin reviewers (who dine in secret) come to the restaurant, and the colleague sabotages Adam, just like Adam did to him. Adam has a huge meltdown; he thinks he's going to get a bad review and lose his chance at that three-star rating, and he goes on a bender. Classic Dark Moment. Even though there's been no conflict yet, it looks like things will turn against Adam and he'll have to struggle to finally win.

Except...

There are still no stakes. Adam's meltdown should have been the end of him, the rock bottom he might not be able to climb back from that would force that internal growth he needs. Adam is supposed to take a drug test every week and talk to the therapist to get his money and keep his restaurant open. It's made very clear that if he screws up, he's out.

And he screws up big time.

Yet *nothing happens* because of it.

He doesn't get tested. He doesn't get into any trouble for falling off the wagon. His therapist never even finds out. The only stated stakes in the movie were fake, as no one ever held Adam accountable for anything he did or did not do. Had that whole aspect not been in the movie at all, it would not have changed anything.

In fact, it turns out that the diners he *thought* were Michelin people were just regular diners. The colleague that sabotaged him didn't do Adam any harm at all (another fake stake), and he's able to get rid of the threat before it can hurt him. So there he is, hungover and feeling crappy, when the real Michelin people show up and he has to serve them.

Which he does and gets his star. Easy peasy.

His only obstacle is that he's hungover after his rough night of drugs and alcohol. Gee, it's a good thing he has an entire staff of highly trained chefs to make the meal under his guidance.

If there's nothing to win or lose, then what happens doesn't matter, and there is no conflict. Even when the story *has* stakes, also make sure the consequences are real and occur if the protagonist fails.

It's always a shame when a story with everything going for it falls flat, especially when a few minor tweaks would have made all the difference. If *Burnt* had embraced the potential conflicts and stakes it had in the story, it would have been a terrific movie. But at least we can all benefit from its mistakes.

A conflict is only as strong as its stakes, so make sure your stakes are personal and dire, and that they come due when the protagonist messes up.

The Tension: The Reason Readers Keep Reading about the Conflict

Tension is a critical aspect of conflict, because if there's no sense of something about to happen, odds are the outcome of what's happening isn't in question. No question = low to no conflict.

Though we often associate tension with characters in danger, it's really just the reader's *anticipation* of something: waiting for the killer to strike, hoping for that first kiss between beloved characters, wondering when a life-changing bit of information will finally be revealed—these are all things that pique readers' interest and keep them reading.

For example:

- ▶ Will the protagonist set off the alarm and alert the security team?

- ▶ Will the protagonist stumble over her invitation to dinner?

- ▶ Will the protagonist uncover the two-headed troll's weak spot?

It's not uncommon for people to say, "There's no conflict" when they really mean, "There's no tension." There's no sense of something about to happen, because there's no fear that the outcome *won't* unfold exactly as expected. Nothing in the scene is going to change that, so there's no sense of conflict.

Except...

Sometimes the conflict itself is just fine, but the outcome is too obvious because the path is so clear. "Press the button or die" isn't a hard choice to make. Everyone is going to press the button. "Press the button to pick which of these two innocent people to kill" is a harder choice, and creates more tension. People will have different reasons for choosing who dies, but it's still probably not a choice that will *really* hook a reader. "Press the button to pick which of your children will die" is an impossible choice loaded with tension. How can a parent possibly pick a child to die?

But tension doesn't have to be life or death to be compelling. Every joke you've ever heard has used tension to capture your attention until the punchline. Movie trailers tease you with details about a movie until you can't wait to see it. Holiday decorations remind you every day about the upcoming date and all the fun (or dread for some) associated with it.

Conflict relies on tension to make readers want to know what happens. Tension relies on conflict to offer enough choices and possible outcomes to make the resolution uncertain. Together, they make readers eager to see how a scene turns out.

Optional: What *Downton Abbey* Can Teach Us about Tension

Even if you don't watch TV, odds are you've heard someone somewhere mention *Downton Abbey*. One of the things that really impressed me about it was the sense of tension. It's a fantastic example of how tension can work without explosions or a hero hanging off the edge off a cliff just by making viewers want to know how the lives of the characters unfold.

Let's examine how *Downtown Abbey* uses tension to strengthen its conflicts.

The story starts with a challenge.

Right away, something has happened and there's a direct consequence to the main characters because of it. In this case, the *Titanic* has sunk and the two main heirs to the lord of the manor have died. No heir = major problem, and the only way for the characters to keep their home and wealth is to marry the eldest daughter to the next heir in line to inherit the estate (clear core conflict with a strong story question—will they marry off the daughter and save the estate?).

How this affects the conflict: A problem with high stakes makes readers curious, and the more unpredictable the outcome, the more tension readers will feel. It clearly matters to the characters in a "life and death" way without actually having someone's life in danger. But their lives will forever be altered for the worse by what has happened. The only way to fix it is to do something the characters would rather not do (more conflict, going against their beliefs). It also leaves questions about the outcome. What will the new heir be like? Will the eldest daughter catch his eye? Will they be able to arrange a marriage or will they be tossed out on their ears if he decides to move into the manor and keep everything for himself? What will they do if that happens?

Starting each scene with a challenge gives the protagonist a problem (and conflict) that has to be solved, and potential outcomes for readers to anticipate (tension).

Things do not go well.

What the characters hope will happen, doesn't. In fact, the opposite occurs. The heir is not at all what the family expected, and he and the daughter do not get along. Not only is the family at risk, but so are the honor and traditions of the estate, which is like a family member to them.

How this affects the conflict: The challenge to overcome is clearly stated and the path to resolve it is laid out, along with the stakes if they fail. It's very clear where the story is going, so it's easy to anticipate possible issues that might occur—both good and bad. The daughter has to win over the heir or the family loses everything. Since the heir doesn't understand what being lord of Downton Abbey means, he's not acting in a predictable way, so tensions are high. Anything might happen and none of it looks good.

Don't give your protagonist a break. Let things *not* go her way, either through her own actions, or the actions of others, and you'll keep tensions high.

Things get complicated.

Once the main storyline is set up, the subplots kick in. The show isn't just about the noble family, but the staff who live and work there as well, since their lives are also affected by what's going on in the main conflict. Every character has goals, hopes, and challenges of their own, and a conflict with at least one other person. Nothing really story-driving, but when combined with everything else going on, there's always *something* that could blow up at any moment. There's tension because there are people who all want different things, and those things could create trouble at any moment. Often, the smaller issues threaten to boil over at the worst possible times for the larger plot, so even these small conflicts can have big effects.

How this affects the conflict: It helps take the pressure off the main story, holds the viewers' attention, and gives viewers even more things to worry and wonder about. These are the subplots and supporting characters of a story, and better still, their actions have consequences and influences on what the main characters are doing. Petty grievances lead to bigger-than-intended problems.

Don't forget to give a few of your secondary and supporting characters problems of their own to deal with (look for characters with problems that also affect the core conflict or protagonist in some way). You don't want to create subplots that require their own book to resolve, but let the other characters have lives of their own that influence what happens around them—they're not just there to prop up the protagonist. Small issues can affect the protagonist and core conflict, and create tension because what the protagonist might need from another character could go against what that character wants. Or what a smaller character does could adversely affect the protagonist.

People make mistakes at the worst possible times.

Tension works when the reader feels that anything might happen at any time and it'll likely be bad. *Downton Abbey* excels at tension-building, because the characters make mistakes—sometimes huge mistakes that threaten everything they want, but also honest mistakes, petty mistakes, and evil, deliberate "mistakes" that are anything but.

How this affects the conflict: It helps keep things unpredictable, and keeps the stakes escalating. It also shows that any character is capable of throwing a wrench into the protagonist's plans, so just because something *looks* like it'll turn out as expected, there's always the chance that someone will make a mistake that changes things.

Let characters act in ways that affect your protagonist when she least needs the distraction or problem. Supporting characters can even help you set up a bad situation that the protagonist can't get into on her own (or create a plot situation that would otherwise feel implausible). Let your protagonist make mistakes, too. Nobody is perfect and people do the right thing for the wrong reasons (or the wrong thing for the right reason) all the time. They even do the stupid thing for the selfish reason.

Not everybody is nice.

Two words for the fans: O'Brien and Thomas. These are two characters you love to hate, but things in the Abbey would go way too smoothly if they weren't there. Yet despite their horribleness, these characters are not really antagonists—they aren't standing in the way of any main characters' goals, just causing general discord that affects everyone in unpredictable ways (they're practically environmental conflicts). O'Brien and Thomas are petty, selfish, and mean-spirited, and they don't care who they hurt to get what they want. They're the stones that cause ripples in the pond that affect everything.

How this affects the conflict: Without a traditional villain antagonist (the antagonist here is a nice guy who just doesn't want what they want), there's no one in the show to root against. These characters take on the role of "characters we hate" so the other characters can shine a bit more. They can also be counted on to make things worse or cause trouble when the plot needs it, and you believe it because they're mean people. Because their actions are deliberate, the consequences have so much more tension and impact than an accident or something contrived for plot reasons.

A nasty character with an agenda can add tension, as readers wonder how far this person will go. They can be unpredictable, vengeful, and petty—and anything can happen with a person like that.

It's all personal.

Every character in this show has something to win or lose, so when things happen, someone is affected by it—usually multiple people in various ways. Nothing happens just to happen.

How this affects the conflict: The sense that even the smallest event can drastically alter someone's life is powerful. It makes readers pay close attention to what's going on, because they know it'll matter somehow, even if it's not clear when it first occurs.

Don't have things happen unless they matter to someone. Even if the problem just affects a small character who interacts with the protagonist only a few times, let that problem have an impact in some way. Let your world and story change the lives of your characters so readers will watch and wonder what each thing will do.

The unexpected, out-of-your-control happens.

For the Abbey, it's World War I. Just when they think things are working out—BAM! The world explodes. It's a nice reminder that sometimes, events larger than the people of the story will occur, and those events can change lives in ways no one ever saw coming.

How this affects the conflict: Sometimes you need outside forces to shake up a story or send it in a direction the characters themselves can't. Plots in the Abbey had played themselves out as far as they could, and forcing new challenges would have felt contrived. Adding a war changes everything; suddenly the petty problems become less vital, and the important problems become more so. This is a particularly helpful device for a series.

Sometimes things *always* going wrong for the protagonist gets tedious and loses impact on the reader. In some cases, you might have to make your protagonist act like a total idiot for her to make a mistake or cause a problem. There's nothing you can do to make things worse or muck up the works, but you still need things to go wrong. An outside event could be the right answer to that.

Even on a smaller level, things can happen in the world or a character's life that are outside her control and have serious effects. It doesn't have to be WWI-level drama to make it work. Something a character couldn't possibly see coming works just as well.

Downton Abbey is a wonderful study of tension and how small things can be just as gripping as huge action events—often more so because they're so personal.

The Environment: The Reason the Conflict Is Harder

The environment is often filled with potential conflict for the protagonist. It might tap into personal fears, such as heights, the dark, or dogs. It might offer physical challenges, such as chasms or dangerous weather. It could even put moral or ethical problems in the way, such as the protagonist risking losing an entire town if she stops to help innocent bystanders during a natural disaster.

For example:

▶ The protagonist who must escape capture will have a harder time doing that in the fields of Ohio than on the crowded streets of New York City.

▶ The protagonist who wants to make a good first impression on her date would have a much tougher time if the sky opened up on the way to that date, and she had to decide between arriving on time and getting drenched.

▶ The protagonist who must use a magic ability to defeat a monster that's rampaging through town will find it much harder if magic is outlawed in that realm.

Unless it's a Person vs. Nature story (where the conflict is all *about* surviving whatever nature throws at the protagonist), the environment can bring additional pressure on the protagonist to make her challenges more difficult. It can intensify internal conflicts or fears, or add an interesting layer to external conflicts that need more depth.

For example:

▶ The protagonist trying to go the straight and narrow might have finally gotten a job at an outdoor event—which gets canceled due to bad weather. Now, she has no way to get the money she needs to pay her rent. Does she resort to crime or does she look for another option?

▶ The protagonist trying to overcome her fear of rejection might find herself on a date doing something she's terrible at, such as miniature golf. Now she's self-conscious about everything she does and feels exposed—the environment makes her uncomfortable, which in turn makes her act in ways that will likely get her rejected.

▶ The protagonist trying to build up her confidence might have to fight a troll in a city filled with innocents, where one wrong move could result in dozens of people dying—so she second-guesses everything she does and doesn't fight at her full ability, too scared to do what needs to be done, and the troll gets away and hurts someone.

Think about the setting and where your protagonist fits in that environment. While you don't want to whip up a tornado just for the drama of it, a story set in Kansas or Oklahoma during tornado season might benefit from some bad weather at the worst possible time.

Optional: What *Sanctum* Can Teach Us about Environmental Conflict

The movie *Sanctum* is a master class in how the setting can affect both the conflict and the tension of a story. Cave diving is an incredibly dangerous activity—so *many* things can go wrong and kill you on a cave dive—and to survive, you might have to make horrific choices. *Sanctum* didn't pull any punches here, and used the environment to make the conflicts the characters faced as challenging as possible.

Here's how they did it:

They created a setting ripe with hazards

Cave diving can be deadly. It's secluded, there's no easy way out, and if something goes wrong you're on your own. In Sanctum, a hurricane traps the characters in a cave, and rising waters force them to find another way out. People are scared, hurt, and tired, which makes them prone to mistakes and bad judgment calls.

How this affects the conflict: If the only way to move forward is to go through more danger, you leave your protagonist little choice but to risk it. If cutting off the escape route isn't feasible, try making one way riskier than the other. The path the protagonist *wants* to take won't work, so she has to go the way she *doesn't* want to go.

Look at your scenes. What kind of environment is your protagonist in? Is she in a place where if something goes wrong she can easily escape or deal with it? This works for emotional escapes too, such as, the protagonist not wanting to face an emotional issue but being in a place where she can't get away from facing it. If you cut off the escape route, the protagonist must deal with the conflict during the worst possible time.

The characters make dumb mistakes

When you ignore the cave diving expert who tells you how to survive the terrible situation you're in, don't be surprised when you die. In an unforgiving environment, one mistake can kill you (which can also be used in our stories). *Sanctum* lets the protagonists get themselves into trouble.

How this affects the conflict: If the protagonist doesn't have all the skills or information needed to get out of trouble, problems *will* develop.

What mistakes might the protagonist make that could cause a catastrophe? A physical mistake that affects a plan? An emotional mistake where she acts without thinking or in a way contrary to what's smart? Perhaps she makes a mental mistake and misreads a situation or vital clue?

The characters *have* to make really awful choices (the good kind)

My favorite aspect of this movie was the truly horrible choices the protagonist had to make to keep as many of his people alive as possible. When something goes wrong in a cave deep underwater, you might have to choose between letting one person die or having many people die. Sometimes, you can't save everyone no matter what you do. If the choices your protagonist has to face are horrible choices, the reader will agonize right along with her.

How this affects the conflict: Not every situation needs to be life or death, but there are plenty of opportunities to choose one person over the other. Make that choice have consequences that add to the problems (potential or real) piling up. Such choices can strongly affect the internal conflict. Is there a line your protagonist refuses to cross? Something she swore she'd never do? How close can the environmental forces push her to that line or that action?

Being in a situation where there is no right answer, and every choice sucks and ends badly for someone, is tense.

Putting characters in an environment rife with potential trouble makes everything they do matter more. One mistake, one slip up and disaster could come crashing down on their heads.

The Different Levels of Conflict

Now that we understand the general problems writers run into with conflict and how it works with its fellow literary elements, let's further explore the different layers of conflict and how they work to build a novel.

What's nice about the layers of conflict is that they work together to create a strong story, so when you understand how to use them, it is easier to develop your novel. The external conflicts create the physical challenges and external obstacles of the plot and the situations that must be resolved to win (however that works in your novel). The internal conflicts provide the internal struggles to make the right choices. They might also create the character arc that shows how the character changes by undergoing the experiences in the novel. The environmental conflict ties the whole team together by giving the plot and the characters a challenging place to work out their differences.

The dictionary definition of conflict nicely illustrates the different forms conflict can take, so let's run through that first:

1. To come into collision or disagreement; be contradictory, at variance, or in opposition; clash.

"Things in opposition" sums up the concept fairly well. The protagonist wants something/believes something/is trying to achieve something, and the antagonist opposes her in some way that requires effort in order to overcome.

For example:

▶ Two politicians both want to be president. (They strive to persuade voters to vote for them.)

▶ Two scientists try to prove opposing theories. (Each works to prove his idea is the correct one.)

▶ A child wants to go to summer camp and Mom says no. (They struggle over freedom vs. parental control.)

At the core, two sides with different ideas about the right thing to do each try to get their way. They're not necessarily enemies (though they could be), just in opposition to each other's goals—only one can succeed.

2. To fight or contend; do battle.

Conflict can, of course, be the physical—a battle to determine the victor. This side versus that side. But the fight doesn't have to be physical. It can be a metaphorical "war."

For example:

▶ War between two villages over water rights in the desert. (They do battle to claim ownership.)

▶ Federal agents raid a drug kingpin's compound. (They do battle to deny or maintain freedom.)

▶ Two lifelong enemies both want to marry the same person. (They do battle to win love.)

The "fighting" type of conflict typically contains a lot of animosity—this isn't a disagreement, it's a battle. The challenge is to overcome or escape the opponent.

3. A fight, battle, or struggle, especially a prolonged struggle; strife.

Sometimes the conflict isn't something that can be decided in one fight, but is, instead, an ongoing problem the protagonist is struggling with or against.

For example:

- ▶ A rebel works to overthrow a tyrannical leader. (She struggles to change things for the better.)

- ▶ A girl battles a terminal illness. (She struggles to survive.)

- ▶ A woman fights to get worker's rights for the employees. (She struggles to improve working conditions.)

The "long struggle" type of conflict typically isn't resolved by winning once, but by repeated victories to change the status quo.

4. Controversy; quarrel: conflicts between parties.

These types of conflict have two sides that disagree, usually over a belief or sense of what's right vs. wrong. You'll often find moral or philosophical issues debated here, and each side struggles to have their way.

For example:

- ▶ A gay male student wants to run for prom queen. (He struggles to change minds.)

- ▶ A husband doesn't want his wife to work. (He struggles to maintain the status quo.)

- ▶ Doctors disagree whether a patient should be treated with an experimental drug. (They struggle over the correct course of treatment.)

This conflict is about convincing the other side that the protagonist is right (or that the other side is wrong), or defying the side the protagonist disagrees with.

5. Discord of action, feeling, or effect; antagonism or opposition, as of interests or principles.

This is more the traditional villain type conflict—the bad guy is actively trying to stop the good guy from winning (or the good guy is trying to stop the bad guy from being bad). The two sides are actively trying to stop each other from succeeding.

For example:

- ▶ A police officer tries to prevent a serial killer from killing again. (She works to stop a murderer.)

- ▶ A local farm boy tries to stop an evil overlord from enslaving the land. (He works to prevent tyranny.)

- ▶ A woman tries to escape from her abusive husband. (She struggles to escape an abuser.)

The conflict here is typically more adversarial, with two sides that can't successfully coexist working to defeat one another.

6. A striking together; collision.

These types of conflicts are often things that can't be avoided, but also aren't personal. Events prevent the protagonist from succeeding, but they aren't being done specifically to that person, it's just bad timing. Natural disasters and forces of nature are good examples here, though any "wrong place, wrong time" situations can also apply.

For example:

- ▶ A girl is the lone survivor of a plane crash in the middle of the ocean. (She struggles to survive.)

- ▶ A man searches for his missing son during a blizzard. (He struggles to find a loved one.)

- ▶ A woman goes to the bank just before it's robbed and she's taken hostage. (She struggles to remain safe.)

Collision conflicts are often unexpected and unavoidable, because they involve forces outside the character's control. The challenge is to endure or survive.

7. Incompatibility or interference, as of one idea, desire, event, or activity with another.

In this type of conflict, the protagonist is often portrayed as her own worst enemy. She wants to live, act, or behave in a certain way, and others in her life are interfering with that and trying to get her to change her ways. It could also cover conflicts between people who have different views on how to accomplish a task, or conflicts people who interfere with each other's goals.

For example:

- ▶ A party girl refuses to acknowledge her self-destructive behavior. (She actively ignores a painful truth.)

- ▶ An obsessed workaholic won't let anyone help him. (He strives to maintain control.)

- ▶ An estranged married couple refuses to compromise. (They fight to have their way.)

Whatever the problem is, the protagonist is making it harder on herself than it needs to be through her actions or refusal to act. The challenge is in doing what she doesn't want to do.

As you can see, conflict encompasses a wide scope of problems and situations, and can be as varied and interesting as you want to make it. But no matter what type of conflict a character faces, it presents a *challenge* in how to resolve the conflict. That challenge leads to a choice on the best course of action, and that choice forces the character to act. And that's good, since those challenges, choices, and actions create the plot (the combination of internal and external conflicts). Without conflicts, the protagonist would have no problems at all (and there'd be no story).

Let's further explore the different aspects of conflict and discuss how writers use them in their stories.

The Core Conflict: The Heart of the Novel

The core conflict is the main problem at the center of a novel. It's what the book is about and the whole reason your characters are putting up with all the terrible things you do to them. If you removed this conflict, you would have no story. This is the conflict (problem) that creates the plot.

In essence, it's what the protagonist needs to do over the course of the novel. Resolving this conflict is the reason the book exists.

Conflicts fall into one of four general categories: Person vs. Person, Person vs. Self, Person vs. Society, and Person vs. Nature (more on these next).

For example:

- A Person vs. Person conflict is typically more plot-focused as two sides struggle over a single goal (the gallant knight trying to stop the evil wizard from enslaving the land, or the FBI agent trying to prevent a madman from blowing up the Super Bowl).

- A Person vs. Self conflict is typically more character-focused as a person struggles over a damaging behavior or belief (the addict trying to get clean, or the consummate bachelor trying to find real love).

- A Person vs. Society conflict typically uses both the plot and character arc as one side struggles to change the society (the girl who believes all women should be able to read, or the man who believes reliance on artificial intelligence will be the death of the human race).

- A Person vs. Nature conflict also typically uses both the plot and character arc as one side struggles to survive against nature (the man trying to save a town from a volcano, or the woman trying to survive abandonment in the desert).

The core conflict is also the conflict the antagonist will be connected to. The core conflict is caused by the antagonist in some way, either deliberately, accidentally, or as a consequence or response to an action.

For example:

- ▶ The murder mystery antagonist causes the novel's conflict by killing the victim (Person vs. Person).

- ▶ The literary fiction antagonist causes the novel's conflict by refusing to seek help for depression (Person vs. Self)

▶ The fantasy antagonist causes the novel's conflict by forcing children to fight to the death in a battle arena (Person vs. Society).

▶ The thriller antagonist causes the novel's conflict by being a volcano that erupts in Los Angeles (Person vs. Nature).

The core conflict typically appears in the novel in one of two ways: A) The protagonist is living her life when something happens to put her into conflict with something else and she can't walk away from the problem; or B) The protagonist acts to obtain a goal and the antagonist prevents her from obtaining that goal. Sometimes there's a blend of the two, with the protagonist acting in a benign way that has unforeseen consequences leading to conflict.

For example:

▶ The protagonist wants to go to school, but only the rich can be educated in her world. (The protagonist causes this by wanting an education in a world she knows won't let her go to school, and the antagonist blocks that goal.)

▶ The protagonist is kidnapped by his ex-wife, and he needs to figure out a way to escape her before she kills him. (The antagonist causes this by abducting the protagonist.)

▶ The protagonist wants to go out with the cute new girl in algebra class, but her brother won't let him near her. (The protagonist triggers the problem, but it's the antagonist who escalates it into a conflict.)

Every novel has one main problem the protagonist is struggling against. The conflict drives the protagonist to act, and it's why the antagonist is acting against her. Whatever that core conflict is determines how you plot (and write) your novel.

Here are the classic story conflict types and how they define the basic conflict structure.

Person vs. Person

This is the most common type of conflict—the classic character against another character, people vs. people, even if those people are non-human. The person standing in the way of your protagonist is another person.

For example:

▶ A wizard wants to kill the hero and enslave the world.

▶ A scientist needs to find the cure and stop the madman with the virus.

▶ An orphan girl needs to save her sister from bad men.

These conflicts are useful for stories that revolve around competing goals, the need to stop something from happening (or cause something to happen), or the need to triumph over another person or group (to name a few).

Key Aspects of a Person vs. Person Conflict

■ The conflict is people up against each other.

■ Each side wants to prevent the other from getting the goal.

■ The antagonist creates the challenges and problems the protagonist needs to overcome, either directly or indirectly.

What makes a problem a Person vs. Person conflict is that the other person has motives to work against the protagonist. For example, the shark in *Jaws* is "in opposition" against Sheriff Brody, but there's no motivation or goal for the shark—it's just a shark doing what sharks do. That's what shifts it into a Person vs. Nature conflict.

A great example of a Person vs. Person conflict is the classic mystery or thriller novel. A crime has been committed (or is going to be committed), and the protagonist is tasked with catching the criminal. James Patterson's Alex Cross must catch the killer and solve the crime, pitting his wits and skills against the murderer's. Lee Child's Jack Reacher must find the criminals and stop them from executing their sinister plan. Both protagonists want to catch and stop the antagonist, and the antagonist will act in ways to escape capture and complete his goal.

Person vs. Person conflicts are usually straightforward (as in, what has to be done), and the problems in the novel arise from the obstacles the antagonist puts in the protagonist's path. There are plenty of twists and turns and interesting things happening between the discovery of the problem and the resolution, but "getting or stopping the bad guy" is usually the goal of the novel—even if the bad guy isn't all that bad.

For example:

- ▶ The head of a rival sorority house wants to close the protagonist's sorority. (The challenge is to stop the rival from getting her way and getting the house closed.)

- ▶ The manager of a local manufacturing plant doesn't want to implement the procedures the new boss wants. (The challenge is to convince the manager that the new procedures will help him and the company.)

- ▶ The mother of the love interest doesn't think the protagonist is good enough for her son. (The challenge is to prove to the mother that the protagonist is worthy of her son.)

The trouble with Person vs. Person conflicts is that their deceptively simple structure means it's far too easy to have the conflict be nothing more than a series of obstacles to overcome. Antagonists act in ways that work in the protagonist's favor, and there's no actual struggle to succeed. As basic as they seem, they can be difficult to do well.

In a Person vs. Person conflict, the antagonist can make or break the story. He's the one creating the situation the protagonist will have to resolve. The harder he makes it, the more she'll have to work to resolve it. But an antagonist who doesn't *really* try to stop the protagonist weakens every victory the protagonist has.

Such antagonists can easily become cardboard clichés, because the focus is on what makes them bad and what they do to hinder your protagonist. They're plot devices to cause the protagonist trouble, not fully developed characters who create challenges by their actions.

The easiest way to avoid this pitfall is to develop your antagonist the same as you would your protagonist, even if the antagonist isn't a point-of-view character. Give him both good and bad traits and a history that shaped him to be what he is in the story. Most important, give him sensible motivations for opposing the protagonist. Let the reader think, "Well, gee, if I were him, I'd probably do that, too."

If you're writing from the antagonist's point of view, making him a real person with real goals also makes it a lot easier to develop strong conflicts, because it isn't about what he's doing to the protagonist—it's about what goal he's trying to achieve and what obstacles are in his way—and those goals just happen to affect the protagonist. Create strong conflicts by making the antagonist more than a plot device that forces your protagonist to do what you need her to do. Make him a character who stirs up trouble trying to get what *he* wants.

Person vs. Self

These conflicts are popular in novels with strong character journeys where the character is at odds with herself and struggling with internal challenges. These conflicts are typically deeply personal and follow a strong character arc, and the protagonist grows from the experience. The person standing in the way of your protagonist is herself, and only through change can she succeed.

For example:

- ▶ Overcoming an addiction problem.

- ▶ Facing her fear of commitment so she can find happiness.

- ▶ Realizing her overblown ego is sabotaging her career and keeping her alone.

Person vs. Self conflicts are good for emotional journeys and stories about personal change. The protagonist's challenge is within. If your protagonist is her own worst enemy, odds are you have a Person vs. Self conflict.

Key Aspects of a Person vs. Self Conflict

- The struggle is internal, but the conflict is externally driven.

- The conflict affects a belief or behavior that needs to change.

- The character cannot obtain the external goal until the internal change occurs.

These stories are a little tougher to write, because the antagonist isn't a person, but a thing to overcome, such as depression, or a self-destructive streak. Technically, there's no "person" plotting against your protagonist—it's a personal belief or behavior holding her back.

But like in any good plot, even if your protagonist is dealing with something internally difficult, she'll still have an external force to reckon with and a goal to work toward. She isn't sitting in a room trying to will herself not to be depressed/grief-stricken/addicted.

Which can make this type of conflict confusing, because while a Person vs. Self conflict drives the *external* plot (the problems come from what the protagonist does), the challenge is about overcoming an *internal* problem (the protagonist's reasons for those actions in the first place).

For example:

- ▶ A Person vs. Self conflict with a protagonist in trouble for stealing from her family to buy drugs is really about her addiction to drugs, not the fact that she stole. The stealing is just how the addiction problem is illustrated. But dealing with that theft is how the addiction problem will be resolved.

- ▶ A Person vs. Self conflict with a protagonist who cheated on her boyfriend so he'd break up with her is really about her fear of commitment and how that's sabotaging her happiness. The cheating is just the external symptom of her internal problem forcing her to examine her life and her behavior.

- ▶ A Person vs. Self conflict with a suicidal protagonist who goes on a dangerous and reckless adventure is really about dealing with the depression, not the adventure itself. Repeatedly putting herself in danger is how she realizes she has a problem and provides insights on how to heal.

The external problem is what the protagonist has to face *because of* that internal conflict. Basically, in a Person vs. Self conflict, the internal conflict is the reason there's an external problem that needs solving, and solving that problem becomes the plot.

That's why a Person vs. Self conflict typically has representatives of the protagonist's problem that work as antagonists. The problem might be the addiction, but *people* are involved somehow in dealing with that addiction. Think of it as a symbolic antagonist.

For example:

▶ The addicted protagonist might have a best friend who drags her out to the club scene every night.

▶ The protagonist who fears commitment might have an unhappy sister in a miserable marriage who constantly tells her, "Never get married."

▶ The arrogant protagonist might have a husband who feeds her ego and tells her she's doing the right thing for her career, even when she's failing.

Let's return to our protagonist with the addiction problem. Say she isn't trying to seek help. She doesn't think she has a problem, she just enjoys cutting loose at the bar to reduce stress. She's still going to have a goal of some type driving the plot, even if that's to get everyone off her back and leave her alone. She will act externally in ways to achieve that goal.

The novel's plot (and core conflict) isn't about "a woman who gets over her addiction." This is her character arc—her inner journey. The problem she's created *because of* that addition, and the actions she takes *because of* that problem, is the plot. If she's not doing anything but being addicted while people try to help until she gets better, you have a premise but no plot yet—because *there is no conflict.*

But the internal conflict is what turns this from a situation into a story. She needs to get over her addiction to get what she truly wants (whatever that is), and by facing the external plot challenges (the conflicts), she'll be forced to make decisions and realize personal truths about herself. These decisions and truths will force her to change her ways and get sober (the internal struggle).

In our story, this woman is on a self-destructive path and needs to get over her addiction. But her party-hearty husband keeps pulling her back into the life. She doesn't think they *have* a problem, it's just fun and games—until something happens that forces her to see how this is bad and she can't keep doing this (the inciting event). Maybe it's an accident, or a death, or a humiliating situation that she can't avoid, but she realizes she needs help. Her behavior is ruining her life.

Problem is, if she quits the life, she also quits the husband, who doesn't want to sober up. But she knows she's not strong enough to stay with him and *not* drink, and he refuses to stop the partying. Now there's external conflict to support that internal struggle, because her choice to sober up has consequences. The plot is about a woman who must escape a marriage that threatens her sobriety. "Leave the husband and get sober" is the goal driving the external plot. "Stop drinking or keep her husband" is the choice driving the internal conflict. "Find the strength to walk away from the addiction ruining your life" is the character arc. Until she stops drinking and finds the strength to get sober, she can't walk away from her marriage. It's all interconnected.

The actual conflict (the Person vs. Self) is getting sober when it will cost her her marriage. That's what's driving the story. But the plot needs an external goal and symbolic antagonist, so the husband becomes the person who represents what the woman is struggling against within herself. Walking away from *him* symbolizes walking away from her need to drink. If the husband left her tomorrow, she'd *still* have a drinking problem. Her issues would not be solved (which is why he's *not* the real antagonist, just a symbol of what she's fighting), even if they might be easier to deal with without him.

The plot of this tale would be her facing situations that will force her to choose which path she'll take—stay with the husband and keep partying, or walk away and get sober. She'll likely have other people or things trying to keep her from her goal of sobriety. Maybe it's her mother who puts pressure on her to stay married and work it out, unaware of the problem. Maybe it's friends who like the husband and don't see the destructive behavior. Maybe it's the bartender who knows what she's going through and thinks her drinking is her way of dealing with a bad marriage.

Let's shift a little and look at a Person vs. Self conflict with a goal that isn't quite as clear as "stop drinking."

Say your protagonist is battling a mental illness. She *knows* she's depressed and *wants* to overcome her depression, so getting healthy is the goal. But what does "getting healthy" entail? What tangible goal can she work toward that also includes the stakes and rising tension that every good story needs? Perhaps she wants to go to her daughter's wedding, or see the Eiffel Tower. She wants to get better because...why? What *specifically* needs to happen to achieve that goal? Just like the symbolic antagonist, what goal represents her "getting healthy."

The depression itself is the conflict, but it's still not doing anything to directly oppose the protagonist. It's a cause of personal problems for sure, but there should also be challenges to overcome that aren't just her illness. *Something she's doing* is in the way of her getting better. Maybe getting healthy means getting treatment, reconciling with estranged loved ones, proving she can hold down a job—to heal, the protagonist will have things to *do*. Therapy. Medication. Lifestyle change. Something.

Thus, the plot of a Person vs. Self conflict comes from *what the protagonist does to both cause and solve her internal problem.*

There's a choice the protagonist has to make, a realization she has to have, sacrifices she has to accept—goals and stakes are all about choices and sacrifices, hence you have plot. The story question driving the novel isn't "Will she get well?" but "Will she figure out and work through the problem so she *can* get well?" It's a subtle difference, but it's the difference between watching someone go through a rough patch and rooting for someone struggling with a problem and wanting them to win. That goal matters, because it's the internal struggle that needs to be resolved.

A Person vs. Self conflict focuses on the things the protagonist needs to do externally to overcome the problem they have internally. The behavior, beliefs, or attitude is the challenge in the way to victory.

Person vs. Society

In this conflict, the protagonist has a problem with something that is status quo in her world. It's not any one person who is causing trouble, it's how things are being done. Everyone is standing in the protagonist's way, but not everyone is at fault.

For example:

▶ A man tries to change an unfair law.

▶ A girl rebels against a tyrannical society that forces kids to fight to the death.

▶ A woman questions why she can't go to school like her brother.

These conflicts revolve around how societal rules or norms affect the protagonist. They're usually unfair and put the protagonist in a desperate or untenable position. Either she has no recourse but to fight back to survive, or she's so angry she strikes back in defiance. If your protagonist is battling something unfair or unjust about the world she lives in, odds are you have a Person vs. Society conflict.

Key Aspects of a Person vs. Society Conflict

■ The protagonist has a different opinion about how society should be.

■ The protagonist suffers for having that opinion.

■ The protagonist fights to change the aspect of society that is making her suffer.

Just like in a Person vs. Self conflict, "society" will have representatives of the problem the protagonist struggles directly against. Some of them will be innocent people just doing their jobs or living their lives (this is the way society is after all), while others will be those creating or responsible for maintaining the society.

There may or may not be a character arc, though it's not uncommon to have the reason the protagonist wants to change the world be connected to an internal belief, such as a need to be free or a desire to survive. Often, the internal conflict is less impactful on the plot than the external conflict (there's a lot of wiggle room here, so don't worry if your story doesn't have a strong character arc—it might not need one).

Although "society" is often portrayed as a large, evil empire, it can also be a smaller group, such as the culture surrounding an office or school. A society can be any group with rules and ways to enforce those rules.

For example, let's say the society is the wilds of high school. There are cliques, social castes, authority figures, outcasts—all the same elements of any other society regardless of its size. This society functions by its own set of rules and cultural norms, and stepping outside those norms results in punishment. The protagonist is a teen girl on the outskirts of popularity who is tired of how the upper-class elite control the school. She decides one day to oppose the most popular girl is school.

Except...

No one wakes up and says, "I think I'll risk everything and try to change the world today." Something happens that makes the status quo unacceptable, and *causes* the protagonist to want to shake things up. Or, she might not start out wanting to change the society, but find a way just to survive it. Whatever the trigger is, it will most likely be deeply personal and a strong enough catalyst to make the protagonist risk her place in that society to try to change it.

Say the protagonist is an average student, and her teachers grade on a curve. In a normal class this wouldn't affect her much, but in this school, the popular kids all get special treatment and automatic As. So on a grading curve that gives the popular kids the As, the actual A students wind up with Bs and Cs, while average students like the protagonist get Cs and Ds. Bad grades hurt her future and can prevent her from going to college or getting a good job after graduation.

Naturally, the protagonist is pissed at how unfair this is.

Then come the plot challenges. Typically, these challenges will be examples of the system and why it's bad—how it hurts the protagonist, the detrimental effect it has on the people she cares about, etc. There will be examples of society trying to reassert control, and you'll most likely have characters filling the roles of society here, with people the protagonist can fight.

Before long the protagonist will find the one person or thing that is the biggest symbol of the society she's trying to overcome, and the personal issues she's trying to resolve. Quite often, destroying, stopping, or altering this person or thing is what brings about the needed change.

By the end, the protagonist has either instigated a change (for good or bad), or has lost to the system. How far to either side this goes depends on the story. The protagonist might blow society out of the water or she might do just enough to start society on a path toward change, even if she fails. Or she might die in utter failure, stoned to death by her neighbors.

A great example of a Person vs. Society conflict is the movie *In Time*. It's a world where people have been genetically altered to stop aging at 25, with a one-year-advance on their lives after that. To continue living, they need to accumulate more time. Working pays them wages in actual time (as in minutes get added to their lives). The rich live for centuries, the poor struggle with just days (or less) left. The protagonist is a poor man named Will who is living hour to hour so to speak.

Will's beef is with the society he lives in. He just wants to live. He isn't trying to bring down a specific person; it's the system he hates. And the system doesn't care one whit about him. The culture and ideals of the world he lives in make it impossible for him to survive let alone be happy. His mother dies in his arms before he can give her more minutes, and he decides to fight the system, and thus fight the society he lives in. The rules of that society are the obstacles and challenges he has to overcome.

In Will's case, the symbolic antagonist is a timekeeper (a cop) who's just doing his job and trying to keep the system running. Even he has no personal stake in Will's problem, but he represents what's wrong and is the person getting in Will's way and helping to drive the plot and provide stakes.

Eventually things get personal, and Will does find a bigger symbol to focus on: a man with enough time to live forever who controls the time banks and the system itself. Bring him down, change the system.

This is a key element to a Person vs. Society conflict—changing the status quo. Whether or not it happens doesn't matter; it's the fight to do so that provides the goals and narrative drive.

A Person vs. Society conflict focuses on the problems the society is creating for the protagonist, and often explores what has to be done to change that society into a world the protagonist wants to live in.

Person vs. Nature

This conflict puts the protagonist up against nature, and that's what's keeping her from her goal. The challenge is against a force of nature that cannot be beaten, but must be endured or survived. There is no person standing in your protagonist's way, only nature Herself.

For example:

▶ A guy is trapped in a blizzard and has to survive.

▶ A city manager fights an unexpected volcano erupting in downtown.

▶ A crew battles a killer storm on the open sea.

Person vs. Nature conflicts differ from the others because often there is no villain to defeat or overcome. Nature conflicts force the protagonist to use her wits, intelligence, and creativity to survive or lessen the severity of the problem.

Key Aspects of a Person vs. Nature Conflict

■ The protagonist fights a natural phenomenon, animal, or creature.

■ The challenge is to survive the conflict, or prevent the severity of the conflict, not necessarily stop it.

■ Facing nature taps into something personal about the characters.

In a Person vs. Nature conflict, someone is often responsible for triggering the natural disaster inadvertently, such as in *The Core,* or putting themselves at risk as in *The Perfect Storm.* Mother Nature is the problem and she doesn't care who or what she's going to destroy. It can be a volcano or hurricane, or something smaller and less aggressive, such as a boy trying to reach the top of Mount Everest (as in Roland Smith's *Peak*).

The easiest example of this is a traditional disaster movie such as *Volcano*. Unbeknownst to the people in the sleepy little town of Los Angeles, an active volcano is about to rise in the La Brea Tar Pits. The protagonist, Mike Roark, is the city's director of city management and it's his job to handle all city-related crises. What begins as a routine earthquake turns into a major event that puts the entire city at risk. To save lives, Mike and his thrown-together-by-chance geologist partner, Dr. Amy Barnes, have to deal with the volcano and the repercussions of its sudden emergence.

If the conflict is large scale, you'll often see several of the lives that will be affected by it. Even if the story is more personal, a one-on-one tale, you often "meet" other people through memories or flashbacks, because these are the people the protagonist is trying to save or get back to. It isn't just about the protagonist and nature; you also see examples of how this is affecting everyone else, usually using the lives of the characters you meet in the first and even second acts. Yes, a volcano is raining lava and ash all over LA, but it's also setting fire to people's homes, sending lava down subway tubes, and putting other folks in danger at the same time.

In *Volcano*, we meet: the lead guy of the city works crew who later sacrifices himself to save a subway driver; the ER doc who's married to the rich developer who indirectly plays a key role in the climax; the geologist's partner, who's funny and whose story doesn't end well; Mike's second in command, who jokes about stealing his job the whole time—until it gets serious and Mike's life is in danger. And for that extra special touch, Mike's teenage daughter just happens to be visiting this week, so he has the added stress of protecting his child.

What makes these personal stories work so well with the conflict is that they intertwine beautifully and show how Nature is going to affect everyone around her. Even if at first you don't know why you're following a particular character, the roles all fit together by the end to help form the solution to dealing with the volcano.

Just like a storm, Person vs. Nature conflicts tend to start out soft and build. It's probably the most obvious example of the traditional goal-problem-disaster structure. The protagonist acts to stop the disaster, fails, things get worse and he has to try something else. This keeps happening until his back is to the wall, lives are at stake, and he has to do something crazy to win. And then you hit him with a major "oh, no!" moment.

In *Volcano*, Mike has a background in handling floods, so he tries flood control measures to dam the flow of lava. This fails. But then Amy realizes the lava is flowing right into neighborhoods and families, so they try collapsing the street to send the lava into the storm canals. This also fails. And then they realize the lava is headed right for the over-packed hospital they've been sending victims to all day (and where that nice ER doc happens to work). Mike decides to bring down the half-built high-rise across the street as a dam and divert the lava away from the hospital. But just as they start detonating the charges, Mike sees his daughter in the blast zone, looking for a lost little boy.

In Person vs. Nature conflicts, things keep getting worse, wearing the protagonist down and sapping all his physical and emotional strength. In order for him to win (survive), you first need to rob him of as much as possible (without getting melodramatic of course).

Surviving the event is almost always at the center of a Person vs. Nature story (even if the protagonist doesn't survive). Survival can be literal, as in a disaster movie, or it can be thematic as in *The Old Man and the Sea*. The old man *could* simply cut the marlin free and head home, but bringing that fish home and not giving in is the whole point. It's all about the protagonist digging deep and finding the strength he didn't know he had to overcome the challenge in front of him.

This is what makes these types of conflicts so compelling. It's not about being smarter than the bad guy, or outmaneuvering the villain; it's about finding the strength within yourself to overcome the threat/event/situation you find yourself in. It's personal perseverance. It's the ultimate underdog story in a way. The "nature" is going to run its course, but how the protagonist handles it is what really matters.

A Person vs. Nature conflict focuses on the struggle to survive or out-last an aspect of Nature, and the lives Nature touches as she passes through.

Whatever conflict you use, the key thing to remember is that no matter who or what is in your protagonist's way, they/it create the challenges that make it harder for the protagonist to resolve the problem. Take out that antagonist and your protagonist can just waltz in and win with no struggle. No evil wizard, no one to fight. No drug problem, nothing to overcome. No unfair law, no reason to protest. No blizzard, nothing to survive.

No core conflict, no story.

External Conflicts: What's Driving the Plot

External conflicts are challenges the protagonist has to physically over-come to resolve the core conflict problem (and all the smaller problems along the way). They're the actions she takes to fix the problems pre-venting her from getting her goal. They're what make up most of the action in the plot, since this is what the protagonist does from scene to scene.

In essence, external conflicts are the physical challenges the protago-nist needs to overcome to resolve a problem.

For example:

- ▶ Protagonist wants to find her missing sister, but someone has stolen the security tapes covering the parking lot she was last seen in.

- ▶ Protagonist wants to impress her date on their trail ride, but she has no idea how to ride a horse.

- ▶ Protagonist wants to surprise his girlfriend with breakfast in bed, but he has to get her kids out of the house first.

External conflicts are based on how the protagonist uses her intelli-gence, skills, and resources (or lack thereof) to overcome an external challenge. The key thing to remember with external conflicts is that resolving them takes action—the protagonist does something. While she might take a moment (or longer) to come up with a plan to overcome the challenge, it's what she *does* that resolves it.

Generally speaking, the scene will unfold like this: The protagonist will be trying to achieve a goal when she's presented with a challenge (she's trying to do something in a scene and something stops her). She'll either react on instinct and try to overcome that challenge, or take time to decide what to do (how much time is up to the writer). The difficulty of the challenge, the level and type of conflict, and the competence of the protagonist determine how that challenge is resolved. What happens at the end of the challenge leads to the next goal of the plot and the next challenge.

This is essentially plotting in conceptual form. Pursue a goal, face a challenge, outsmart or overpower it, proceed to the next challenge with a new goal.

Of course, while most external challenges just require skill, strength, or intelligence to overcome, others will be much harder to resolve due to personal issues. This is where the internal conflicts kick in, so let's look at those next.

Internal Conflicts: Making the Protagonist's Life Harder

Internal conflicts are the emotional, ethical, or mental struggles a character faces while trying to decide what to do about an external problem. The challenge isn't a physical thing in the way, but a struggle within the protagonist to make the right choice.

In essence, it's the mental and emotional debate the protagonist needs to have in order to resolve an external problem.

For example:

▶ Protagonist wants to save her missing sister, but doing so will reveal a secret she can't afford to have known.

▶ Protagonist wants to be loved, but her refusal to compromise keeps her alone.

▶ Protagonist wants to romance his girlfriend, but he doesn't want to risk making her kids mad and their not liking him.

An external task that's easy to complete can be made difficult by adding an emotional roadblock. What needs to be done is clear, but the protagonist doesn't want to resolve it that way for personal reasons. Either the right choice has consequences she doesn't want to suffer, or there is no good choice—whatever she does has serious ramifications.

Internal conflicts are based on who the protagonist is and what has happened to her in her life, and this past makes it harder for her to make decisions and resolve her external challenges. They typically come from the morals and ethics of the character, and more often than not, choosing one side negates the other and the protagonist can't have it both ways.

Common places for internal conflict:

A contradiction to the belief system: What a character thinks is true affects behavior. If the right choice contradicts what the protagonist "knows" is true, she probably won't choose it. At the very least, she'll struggle and do some serious soul searching to resolve that conflict and make that choice. For example, a woman who has been badly mistreated by men her entire life will very likely believe that all men are bad people not to be trusted. So if she has to make a decision based on trusting a man, there's a good chance she'll have trouble making it.

An act against morality and ethics: How a character believes other people should be treated will also affect how she makes a decision. For example, if she believes killing is wrong, any choice that requires killing someone (or even killing an animal) will be met with fierce resistance. The character's morality is rooted in her personal rules and laws of acceptable behavior. But if killing is the only way to save someone she loves, or prevent something terrible from happening, she might be tempted. Doing a bad thing for a greater good can be a persuasive argument.

A crisis of conscience: Sometimes a character wants to do things she knows is wrong. For example, it might be a minor transgression, such as lying to a friend to get out of going somewhere when she's tired and wants to stay home, or a major breach of ethics, such as stealing from her employer because he cheated her out of a promised bonus. What she wants to do goes against what she knows is right, and she's doing her best to rationalize why it's okay to do it anyway.

When fear sways better judgment: Even the best person can act badly out of fear. If a character is focused on survival or avoiding a terrible fate, she might make bad decisions or go against her morality. For example, a character might stay quiet about a belief and not stand up for someone being mistreated out of fear she'll be attacked in turn. Or, she might lie or agree to something she knows is wrong to keep something of value to her (such as a job).

Embarrassment or shame: Shame is a powerful emotion. People can ignore their ethics and personal beliefs if it means saving themselves from a terrible secret being revealed. (Think back to middle school or high school.) They'll act to avoid standing out or looking foolish, which can keep them from doing the right thing at the right time to prevent a problem. Someone who witnessed a crime while doing something embarrassing isn't likely to tell anyone for fear their own transgression will be exposed.

Internal conflicts are great opportunities to put the protagonist in the hot seat and force her to decide who she is and what she stands for. How far is she willing to go to help a friend? What will she risk? What does she value? Her struggles while making a decision shows readers who she really is as a person.

Environmental Conflicts: The World Really *Is* Out to Get You

Conflict also exists in the world *around* the characters which has nothing to do with them personally—it's just the inherent conflict of the world. The setting can be rife with problems that prevent your protagonist from solving her challenges and even add to her internal conflicts.

Getting food when you live in a big city is different from getting food if you're lost in the woods with no gear or survival training. Dealing with a backstabbing co-worker during a team-building ride in a hot air balloon is more problematic when you're terrified of heights.

In essence, environmental conflicts are the issues and situations that make it harder to solve the problems and face the challenges (internal and external conflicts) of the novel.

For example:

▶ Protagonist gets evicted from her boarding room and has no place to stay, but staying out in the open after dark will likely get her assaulted, captured, or even killed. (The world itself is dangerous and those dangers have to be dealt with before the protagonist can fix her story problems.)

▶ Protagonist goes home to visit family, because her sister is getting married, and she knows everyone will hound her about her love life. (The protagonist's life is a constant reminder of her problem and won't let her walk away from it.)

▶ Protagonist lives in a small town where everyone knows everyone, so the killer hears about her every move. (The setting and people in it add another layer of difficulty to an existing problem.)

Let's say you have a scene where you want your protagonist to feel uncomfortable because she's confronting a coworker who just stabbed her in the back at work over a promotion.

Where would you set it?

The most obvious choice is at work, since that's where she interacts with this person. She'd likely do it somewhere familiar to her, because she'll want a position of strength for this confrontation. But that means she'll be in familiar and safe territory, which will probably keep her calm and lessen her apprehension of this meeting. Being calm and feeling safe will not add conflict to this scene, so the setting is doing nothing to help it.

Let's move this meeting to a location that puts the protagonist at a disadvantage, so the stakes go up and the tensions are raised. Instead of work, let's choose a place that makes her uncomfortable and let the setting reflect the emotions we want both the character and the reader to feel.

For example, if she wants to confront the coworker in private, let's force her to confront her coworker in a public place where anyone might overhear. If she's a recovering alcoholic, we'll send her into a bar where drinks are flowing heavily. If she dislikes kids, we'll make her attend a birthday party for twenty ten-year-olds. Whatever triggers her discomfort is a potential setting, because it will add another layer of difficulty to her objective.

If we use the environment to push the emotions of the protagonist to new heights, we'll make her goals harder to accomplish, which adds conflict and raises tensions, since it's far more likely something will go wrong.

Sometimes, the world really is out to get you, and just getting through the day is a huge challenge. Take advantage of what your environment can do to layer in emotions, create conflict, and make a character really work to resolve her challenges.

Together They Are Stronger

Employing layers of conflict also helps with plotting, because you'll have multiple options for creating unpredictable outcomes (and provide your characters challenges) in every scene in your story. Unpredictability keeps readers guessing and turning the pages.

Common Reasons for Weak or No Conflict

Conflict issues most often come down to a lack of goals, motivations, or stakes. Frequently, you'll see several of these at once, since weak conflict in one area can affect the entire novel. With a weak conflict, the protagonist and other characters drift through the plot doing what they're told, but they don't truly care what happens. They're acting because the author tells them to.

This is why you can have an action-packed novel and still get rejected due to a "lack of conflict." It's also why you can have an emotional, soul-searching saga that puts your readers to sleep because "nothing happens." Action and emotion aren't enough if the conflicts aren't backing them up. They're just "stuff in the way" obstacles.

By now you should have a solid handle on the various types of conflict and how those conflicts work with, and are affected by, other writing aspects (such as goals and stakes). Let's look at the most common problems writers run into when creating (or failing to create) conflict.

The Conflict Doesn't Drive the Plot

Resolving a conflict is what a plot is all about, so a problem with the goal is one of the more common reasons for conflict troubles. Goal issues include:

There Are No Goals

Since conflict is the challenge preventing the protagonist from getting what she wants, wanting something is pretty critical. No goal = no conflict. If the protagonist isn't trying to achieve or obtain something, there's no reason to throw challenges in her way. If you do anyway, you usually wind up with a novel about someone who wanders around aimlessly until something makes her stop and solve a random problem.

For example:

- ▶ A random person asks the protagonist for help stealing a rare coin and she agrees (even though there's no reason for her to help and she doesn't actually want the coin).

- ▶ The protagonist's plane is hijacked and she sits quietly the entire flight, but is then taken hostage by the hijackers and dragged all over the city from one danger to the next as police chase them (plenty of conflict for the police and hijackers, but the protagonist is just along for the ride and does nothing).

- ▶ The protagonist has lucky encounter after lucky encounter that lead to her getting a big reward at the end (even though she never wanted that reward and did nothing to earn it).

Characters "swept up in danger" or "swept away by events" *can* work to get the protagonist *into* trouble and start the story (they make good inciting events), but after that, the protagonist needs goals to work toward and challenges to overcome or there will be no conflict.

If you can't pinpoint the main goal—the one thing that has to be resolved or the book won't work (remember the core conflict?)—odds are that's why the novel feels like it has no conflict.

If you do have a solid core conflict goal, then look at what's preventing the protagonist from obtaining this goal. Who or what is the antagonist? Who is logically in opposition and creating the challenges the protagonist must face and struggle with to resolve the goal? If you see no antagonist, add that opposition.

If the main goal is working and you have the right antagonist, then the problem might lie with how your plot resolves your core conflict. Look at each scene and determine if it has a goal and if those goals are working to lead the protagonist to the climax of the novel (the resolution of that main goal). Look for ways to make the protagonist more active in solving problems and wanting to solve those problems.

Let's look at another common goal issue in a weak conflict:

There's Only One Major Goal

Sometimes the problem isn't a lack of goals, it's that every single goal in the novel is the same one, and the path to getting that goal is too clear. It's obvious where the plot is going and what's going to happen to get there, and nothing in the protagonist's way feels like a real problem.

For example:

▶ The protagonist must stop a biological outbreak before it escapes the lab, and the goals are a series of situations with her trying to prevent the virus from getting loose in some fashion (so the conflict is just her delaying when the virus gets free until she finds the right way to stop it, but nothing that would create any expectation that something else is going to happen before the end of the novel).

▶ The protagonist needs to dry out in rehab, and the goal of every scene is her fighting against the people trying to help her until she gives in (so there's no sense of her learning or overcoming anything, she just stops fighting when the book is over).

▶ The protagonist is trying to find an object and every goal is another lead to where that object might be, but it's never there (so nothing the protagonist does has any actual effect on the plot until the final clue that leads her to the object).

The problem with "one-problem novels" is that every scene is basically the same scene with different details. It feels like there's plenty of conflict as each scene will have a goal, a challenge, and stakes, but when you look closer, not a single challenge advances the story or plot. The only possible outcomes are "yes" and "no." Yes, the protagonist gets the goal, or no, the protagonist does not get the goal.

Since the protagonist can't get that "yes" until the climax, every goal ends with "no" and basically starts over. Nothing that happens matters, because only the last goal advances the plot, and even then, it's usually not a real conflict because it doesn't matter if the protagonist fails—that's been proven over and over again throughout the novel. If failing the last ten times didn't matter, the final try won't either.

However, if each failure teaches a lesson, and the protagonist is learning from those failures, then the loss means something. It's not just a pointless roadblock, but a challenge that results in furthering the character arc or emotional journey. A good example here is every sports underdog story, such as *Rocky* or *The Mighty Ducks*. These teaching moments are what separate a "one-problem story" from a compelling story arc.

Mysteries are another good example. Yes, there is one main problem—catch the killer—but not every scene involves the protagonist against the killer and the killer getting away. The goals are varied in the pursuit of the killer, so there are various problems to overcome before the killer is caught.

Conflicts with a "one problem" issue often have a lot of exciting scenes that seem as if they're moving the plot, but nothing changes from the protagonist's experiencing them. If you took out random scenes in the novel, losing those scenes wouldn't affect the outcome of the plot. Since the goals don't cause anything to change, cutting several of them doesn't affect much of the overall story.

Randomly reorganizing the scenes is another way to test your goals—would it change the story much if the scenes unfolded in a different order? Sometimes we want to keep these scenes because they contain information we think is relevant to the plot—sometimes it is, other times it isn't. Cutting the scene would lose that important information, but that's all that would be lost because the scene does nothing to drive the plot. Odds are that information could easily be added elsewhere.

And then there are the novels that try to do *too* much.

There Are Too Many Goals

These novels have multiple protagonists, multiple problems, multiple conflicts to resolve, and every character pursues a different goal. There are so many goals and conflicts that nothing stands out as the core conflict or what the novel is about.

For example:

▶ Protagonist A wants to save her father from the mines, protagonist B wants to avoid getting sent to the mines, protagonist C wants to keep his job running the mines, protagonist D needs the mines to maintain her wealth and power, and protagonist E wants to shut down the mines to stop an environmental disaster that will kill everyone. (Sure, everything revolves around the mines in some way, but exactly what is this book about? And what do any of these goals have to do with each other aside from being loosely connected to the mines?)

▶ Protagonist A wants to meet someone and fall in love, protagonist B wants to get a promotion so he can afford to get a boat and see the world, protagonist C wants to find a way to manage four kids by himself, and protagonist D wants to leave her abusive husband once and for all. (While these are all potential conflicts, what exactly is this novel about? How are these goals leading toward a single larger conflict that connects them?)

▶ The protagonist wants to find out the truth about her mother, but she also wants to get into the King's Guard, and then there's her dream of competing in the Regional Jousting Games. But before she can do any of that, she has to help this cute guy she met at the inn find the Amulet of Viznet, otherwise his entire village will be eaten by dragons. And she'll also have to figure out how to defeat the dragons, while falling for the cute guy, who has a dark secret that might have something to do with her mother. (Any one of these could fill a novel, but throwing them all into a single story pulls the protagonist in too many directions, so it's not clear what actually matters here.)

Strong, clear goals lead to strong, clear conflicts, so think about what your protagonist wants in every scene of the novel, and how that smaller goal contributes to the larger core conflict.

The Readers Don't Care about the Conflict

No matter how strong the conflict is, if readers don't care about it, it won't make them want to read the story. Most often this is due to a lack of stakes, or a lack of choices about what happens. Stakes issues include:

There Are No Stakes

For readers to care about a character's problem, there needs to be a consequence that makes resolving that conflict critical—the stakes. "There's not enough conflict" often translates into, "It doesn't matter if these people win or not." Nothing happens if they fail.

For example:

> ▶ If the protagonist doesn't pass the test, she'll have to take it again at a later date. (So why worry about her failing the first one?)

> ▶ If the protagonist doesn't break into the suspect's home, she'll have to find the evidence somewhere else. (If she can get the evidence elsewhere, why does she have to risk breaking into this house?)

> ▶ If the protagonist makes a total fool of herself at the company picnic, she'll get laughed at on Monday. (Which won't be fun, but there's nothing here that shows why that would be particularly bad for this person.)

Stakes tell readers how important the protagonist's goal is, which makes them worry about overcoming the challenge to get that goal. The stronger the conflict, the higher the stakes should be. Failing should matter and cost the protagonist something she'd rather not lose.

For example:

- ▶ If the protagonist's ability is exposed, she'll be used as a weapon against her own people.

- ▶ If the protagonist remains inflexible, she'll spend her life alone and miserable.

- ▶ If the protagonist doesn't risk her family's security, a killer will go free and escape to kill again.

Problem is, sometimes you can have what feels like high stakes and readers *still* don't care. This often equates to the dreaded, "It was well written, but it just didn't grab me," type feedback. It sounds crazy, but this is often due to the stakes being too *high*, giving the conflict nothing to build toward. The most common offender here is death.

Death is a lousy stake. How many protagonists actually die by the end of the novel? Almost none, and readers know this, so threatening the hero with death isn't as dire at it ought to be. Same with killing large numbers of faceless people. Right this second, people all over the world are facing conflicts that could cost them their lives. Do you care? Probably not. Faceless people don't affect us the same way as people we know. Yes, we care in a humanitarian way, but it doesn't keep us from living our lives, and it won't make us care about a bunch of story people we don't know.

Writer: My hero must stop the evil wizard before he destroys the land and kills everyone!

Reader: So? Why should I care?

And the reader is right—why should anyone care about this? There's no conflict, just a bad guy being bad and a good guy trying to stop him because one is good and one is evil.

However...put something personal at risk that the protagonist cares about, and make it clear that those consequences can and will happen if the hero fails, and suddenly readers are more interested.

Writer: My hero is forced to choose which friend she must sacrifice to stop an evil wizard from destroying the land.

Reader: Oooh, tell me more.

Stopping the evil wizard from destroying a land readers have never seen isn't nearly as compelling as watching the protagonist struggle to decide which of her friends she must send on a suicide mission to stop that wizard.

Now let's look at a situation that's pretty far from life or death and hardly a story-driving conflict:

Say little Joey is home with the babysitter, who wants him to finish his dinner before bed. The babysitter demands he eat his broccoli. He refuses; she insists. There's no *compelling* conflict here, even though there is a conflict over the consumption of broccoli. It doesn't *really* matter if Joey eats his broccoli. Nothing will happen to him or the babysitter if he doesn't. The babysitter saying, "Eat your vegetables," doesn't get much of a response. "Eat your vegetables or else" is a little better, because the "or else" could be something bad. The conflict (consumption of vegetables), forces the child to make a choice (say yes or refuse), and the "or else" is the consequence for that decision. How much readers care about this conflict depends on those consequences.

Right now, nobody cares about this conflict.

But what if Joey is highly allergic to broccoli? He tells the babysitter this fact, but she doesn't believe him. Joey knows if he eats that broccoli, he's going to wind up in the hospital sick as can be. And after countless refusals, the babysitter is not above holding Joey down and shoving that broccoli down his throat. She's a lot bigger than poor little Joey, so the chances of Joey avoiding his broccoli are slim. There are even stakes for the babysitter, because putting a kid in the hospital will really cut into her babysitting gigs.

Curious what happens now? Probably, because the stakes are higher. Joey eating his vegetables has *real* consequences to both sides. The conflict matters.

Stakes don't have to be huge. They just have to be interesting enough for readers to want to see how the conflict turns out.

Even when the stakes *are* high, if the outcome of the conflict is obvious, readers might not care about it.

There Are No Choices

Choices drive every single conflict in a novel. The protagonist wants something (the goal), something is in the way (the conflict), and she must make a choice about what to do (to get what she wants). The opposition might be direct or indirect, but it's the challenge faced and the choices made to achieve that goal that make the conflict (and the novel) work.

If the choice is obvious and no one would ever choose the other options, it's not really a choice, and any conflict in making that choice goes right out the window.

For example:

▶ Protagonist has to choose between going on an adventure that could change her life or staying home watching TV all weekend.

▶ Protagonist has to decide between helping the bad guys break into the boss's office or refusing and having them kill her child.

▶ Protagonist has to decide if he should date the wonderful physical therapist he met at the gym or the delightful attorney he met at the dog park.

Making a decision is one of the most important things your characters will ever do. Readers turn the page to see what happens next, and decisions are all about the "next." As long as they *care* about that choice.

"Should I have the eggs or the cereal?" is a choice, but no one is going to stay up late to see how *that* turns out. Because the other half of choosing is the fear that you're making the wrong choice (the struggle side of internal conflict).

Now, here's where it gets tricky.

The characters will have their own concerns, but what makes their choices matter is how *readers* feel about it. If readers care about the outcome of a choice, that choice matters to them even if it doesn't matter to the character (who might not realize the importance of the choice yet). If readers don't care, no matter how important that choice is to the character, it won't matter to readers.

If a choice is a core conflict choice, then it should have major consequences. If the entire book is *about* that choice (such as a romance or character-driven novel), there has to be high stakes for making it. If the choice isn't that important to the overall story, then it can have lesser consequences—but honestly, if the outcome doesn't matter, why have it in the book in the first place? The choices don't have to all be bad options, but they should have a consequence that matters to readers and characters.

Let's look at a very common choice in fiction—choosing between two romantic options. If the choice is, say, between two men, and there are no consequences aside from hurting one man's feelings, the stakes aren't high enough to carry a whole novel—because it isn't a choice readers are likely to care about. Sure, readers will have a preference between these two men, but unless more is going on in the novel, they can just flip to the back and see who wins.

As a core conflict, a choice between two good things with no consequences for making that choice is probably not going to hold a reader's interest. But as a subplot, or in conjunction with an internal conflict, it *can* be an effective choice and provide higher stakes—but only if it also has the potential to cause trouble for your protagonist. And this is key.

Let's go back to those two men...If hurting one of them was all the consequence the protagonist had to worry about, so what? Harsh as that sounds, whoever "loses" will likely just go on with his life and find a much better gal than the one who dumped him. As for the woman, nothing bad is going to happen to her for breaking his heart. It's probably not going to hurt her in the long run, even if she does feel bad about it for a while.

If, however, the man was so upset he killed himself, that's a pretty serious consequence to her actions that she'll have to carry around the rest of her life (if a clichéd one). If he decided to make the protagonist's life miserable in revenge, that would cause her trouble. If the man she dumped was her new boss's brother, she might be in a world of hurt at that new job.

The consequence doesn't even have to be this overt, and might have subtle ramifications for the protagonist. It can cause emotional troubles—it can make her so guilt-ridden it keeps her up nights and causes a ripple effect. It might make her realize the callousness of her actions and trigger a change to be more compassionate toward people. She might choose not to make a choice and get herself into real trouble by continuing to date both men.

Whatever the choice, it should have the power to affect your protagonist in some way (usually adversely), even if that problem is down the road a bit. If there's nothing to gain by overcoming a challenge, there's no point in winning or seeing who wins and how. Just look at all the fans who leave a sporting event before the end when it's clear who's going to win. The conflict is no longer important because the outcome is obvious.

There's No Point to the Conflict

Sometimes a conflict occurs because the writer feels the scene needs "more conflict." But random conflicts usually feel, well, *random*. Just making the situation harder seldom makes it a more compelling problem, and it can even verge on melodrama if you take it too far.

For example:

- ▶ The protagonist is running from the hitman when a car comes out of nowhere and crashes into her (and it's just some poor drunk who shouldn't be behind the wheel).

- ▶ The protagonist is late for a huge meeting that could earn her the needed promotion when the bank she's in gets robbed (and this has nothing to do with the story).

- ▶ The protagonist gets into a big fight with her spouse over something irrelevant to the plot, and the argument is resolved before they go to bed (and it had zero effect on the plot or story).

This is why antagonists with plans and goals of their own lead to much stronger conflicts, even if readers never see inside their heads. Their plan is grounded in strong motivations and goals just like the protagonist's, so when the protagonist is trying to solve one problem, the antagonist is chugging along on his own causing trouble there or somewhere else. When "random" things happen, there's a reason.

Everything Is Too Easy to Overcome

Failure to care can also happen when it's too easy to overcome a challenge. The problem might look insurmountable, but the protagonist completes the task without any trouble at all. Sometimes these not-challenges are especially problematic, because they *look* as though they have everything a strong conflict needs. The only thing missing is the actual conflict part. Make the conflict a *real* challenge and it'll work just fine.

For example:

- ▶ The protagonist must face a labyrinth of traps to escape the evil wizard's dungeon— but she figures out the solution to each and every trap on the first try and gets away without a scratch.

- ▶ The protagonist terrified of public speaking must give a presentation to an auditorium of co-workers at the last minute—but once she starts talking the words flow right out and she nails it.

- ▶ The protagonist must find the cure to a deadly virus—and all it takes is one long night in the lab to find it.

No matter what stands between the protagonist and her goal, she overcomes it with little to no effort. Sure, she wins, but she doesn't earn the victory, so readers feel unsatisfied with the conflict.

Special note about easy wins: Sometimes an easy victory is just that, but other times the victory can make the entire scene (or novel) feel contrived. We'll talk more about that next.

When readers want to see how the protagonist overcomes a challenge, they care about the outcome of that conflict.

The Conflicts Are Contrived

Contrived plots not only stretch plausibility, they also hurt an author's credibility with readers. Readers trust us to tell them a solid tale, and they lose that faith if we cheat by forcing events to unfold that allow our protagonists to win with no effort.

Some argue that every story is contrived, because as writers, we manipulate what happens to tell our tale. On one hand this is true, but it's *how* we manipulate that determines how contrived a story reads. For example, if we show our protagonist coming home from her karate class in the first few pages, it's no surprise to readers when she's able to fight off an attacker later. But if we mention she's a black belt *after* the attack has been thwarted—or worse, comment that, "It was a good thing she'd just earned that black belt" *during* the attack, then the scene will likely feel contrived. The vital skill wasn't in the story until it was needed.

That's the key difference between plots that feel contrived and ones that feel plausible. Coincidences happen, and it's not uncommon to have one or two occur in a story to make the whole thing work, but they typically work best when the coincidence is what brings people together or triggers the novel's conflict, not the force behind getting the protagonist out of it.

General rule of thumb: If the contrivance hurts the protagonist, it's usually okay. Contrivances that help the protagonist usually feel forced or overly convenient.

Let's look at some of the more common situations that could mean a contrived plot:

The Protagonist Is Incredibly Lucky

The incredibly lucky protagonist is probably the most common way we force our plots to unfold the way we want them to. Whatever needs to happen for the plot to move forward does, even if the protagonist doesn't do anything but show up. These situations can feel perfectly fine to us as writers, because the information and forward movement is what needs to happen for the scene to work—the problem is that the protagonist did nothing to earn it, so there's no conflict. And since a key piece of information often drops in the protagonist's lap out of the blue, there's no goal either, and probably no stakes.

Lucky breaks include:

Always being in the right place to overhear vital information: You can get away with one of these in a book, but more than that stretches credibility—especially if there's no reason for the protagonist to be where she hears the information.

Taking a wrong turn or getting lost puts the protagonist where she needs to be: These are particularly tricky, because they commonly come after a harrowing escape or chase scene that feels exciting, so it does seem like the protagonist "did something" to get there. But all she really did was happen across the right place by sheer luck, not because she worked to get there.

Random people give the protagonist what she needs with no effort on her part: This is one of the more common contrivances in a novel, because the protagonist is technically working toward her goal—it's just that everyone she speaks to gives her what she needs without her having to do anything but show up. For example, she's at a dead-end in her investigation and stops at a random diner for lunch, but while talking to the waiter, he just "happens to know" exactly the information she was trying to discover all day.

A problem is solved out of the blue right when the protagonist needs it: The most common example here is the person with money trouble who receives an inheritance right when she needs it, but any unexpected "rescue" can be a problem. The protagonist finds herself in a situation that will take a lot of effort to get out of, but someone or something appears and either solves it, or makes it trivial to obtain success.

Bad guys constantly make mistakes that aid the protagonist: The poor, unlucky villain who never catches a break falls into this category. The reason the protagonist wins is because the antagonist messes up; it's not due to any effort on the protagonist's part. What's worse is that often the only way the protagonist *can* win is if the bad guys fail, so it's not really a win. Had the protagonist not been there, the same outcome would have occurred.

If luck always breaks *for* the protagonist (even bad luck), then you might have a contrived conflict on your hands.

There Are No Motivations to Act

In a contrived conflict, characters rarely have a plausible reason to do what they're doing. If a scene requires everyone to act antagonistically toward one another, they will. If a scene requires them to be suspicious, they are. If a scene requires them to run off into the desert on a hunch, off they go. So you wind up with scenes that leave readers asking, "Why in the world are these people doing this?"

For example:

▶ The protagonist believes every word from someone she has zero reason to trust and a list of reasons not to trust (except the plot says *this* time she can, because this needs to happen for the story to move forward).

▶ The protagonist completely changes her opinion about something with no reasons to explain why (except that she must feel that way for the scene to work).

▶ The protagonist is prophesied to stop the antagonist, so the antagonist sends his minions to kill her—even though the protagonist has no clue who the antagonist is and has no reason to stop him *until* he attacks her first and forces her to fight back (which causes the conflict the antagonist wanted to avoid, creating the situation and fulfilling the prophecy).

Whatever the scene is, the situation is twisted so events turn out how the writer wants them to, even if there's nothing in the story that would logically lead to that situation or outcome. The scene might contain all the right pieces to create conflict, but without plausible motivations for the challenge, the conflict feels like a huge coincidence at best, a contrived plot at worst.

Contrived motivations include:

Characters who act "on a whim" or have and do the exact thing needed to move the plot forward: Anytime you use the words "suddenly," "on a whim," or "on a hunch," stop and make sure there's a logical reason for the character to be doing whatever she's doing. Actions triggered by following logical clues and plausible segues are great and lead the protagonist where she needs to go, but be wary when the only reason she acts is due to a wild hunch based on nothing.

Characters who have "sudden suspicions" about someone they have no reason to suspect—and they're right: While very similar to the "whim" issue, this one is created when a character has trusted or believed another for a large portion of the book, and then out of the blue, the protagonist gets suspicious. The character has done nothing to make anyone suspicious, though the protagonist thinks, "They've been acting weird lately," and acts against them in some way—most commonly by following them, searching their belongings, or preparing for an "inevitable betrayal" they had no reason to think was coming. Naturally, these sudden suspicions always turn out to be correct.

A test for plausible character motivations is to simply ask, "Why shouldn't my protagonist just walk away?" If the only answer is, "Because then there's no one to stop the bad guy," odds are there's no reason for the protagonist to act other than that the plot requires it. When you think about it, the whole point of the book is to stop that bad guy (however that appears in your story), but it's the *why* that makes readers want to see how *this* character resolves *this* conflict. The protagonist should have a reason for not walking away and letting someone else deal with the problem.

Things Feel Too Convenient

While coincidences *do* occur in real life, when there are too many of them in a novel it steals all the credibility from the story. The conflicts are there only because the antagonist needs to oppose the protagonist at that moment, and whatever it takes to get those characters into that situation is what happens—even if there's zero groundwork laid to do it.

For example:

▶ A character decides on a whim to search through the company's personnel files and then finds the person they needed to find to move the plot forward.

▶ A character treats the protagonist with undue hostility for no reason and they're the person actively keeping her from the goal.

▶ The protagonist is stuck with a ticking bomb, but somehow has not only the right tools, but the right knowledge to disarm it—even though nothing was ever mentioned before that she had these skills.

Readers are willing to suspend disbelief for a few small coincidences—that's just the nature of novels, especially to set up the premise—but when the critical elements of the plot hinge on characters acting in ways they never would (or never have so far), readers can feel the author pulling the strings and forcing the characters into predetermined roles, which prevents the story from unfolding organically.

Some common coincidences include:

An unmentioned-before-it-was-needed detail provides the reason for something to happen: Like the karate example from above, we backfill the necessary reason so the plot works the way we want it to. Often, these slip in because we realize we need a reason for X to happen when we're writing it, so we create a reason on the fly without ever laying the groundwork. Luckily, these contrivances are easy to fix—just slip in the information before it's needed.

People running into each other when there's no reason for them to do so: Sometimes we need to have two people randomly bump into each other at the right times. When the groundwork has been laid to show that it's plausible for this to happen, it feels like a natural coincidence and readers read right past it. But when there's no way these two people would ever be at this location, let alone at the same time, it's going to stretch credibility. But be extra careful here—it's easy to *create* a contrivance while trying to establish a reason for them to meet in this way.

The conflict should be a result of the protagonist's goal and the choices she made to achieve that goal. If the protagonist chose to ignore A to deal with B and now A is coming back to bite her in the butt, it'll feel plausible to the plot. Or maybe she tried to fix X and that made B happen. But if B happened out of the blue, or due to a *lot* of carefully orchestrated coincidences, it'll feel contrived to readers.

Coincidences *do* happen, and plots *are* all about getting the characters to do what we want them to, but the beauty of a good novel is that it doesn't feel like we're behind it pulling the strings.

In a novel, we have to manipulate events a *little* to tell the story we want to tell. The trick is to nudge the characters and events just enough to direct the story without forcing the story, or drawing the reader's attention to what we're doing.

The Conflict Is *Just* a Delay Tactic

An obstacle course has plenty of obstacles to get in the way, but do you really want to watch someone running it for hours upon hours? I doubt it. After the runner's skill is established, there's nothing to hold your attention or make you care. You know how every obstacle will be overcome, and even if you don't, you know it'll be circumvented and the runner will reach the ending.

Obstacles do not equal conflict.

I've read (and written if I'm being honest) plenty of scenes where the "big problem" was to get past an obstacle in the way. It might be getting around a bad guy, or scaling a giant wall, or solving a puzzle, but the goal of the scene was to overcome the obstacle in the protagonist's path. Technically, "something in the way" is conflict, but it's not a challenge that requires a choice or has any stakes, so it does nothing more than delay the protagonist from getting to the next problem.

In novels with weak to no conflict, that next problem is just *another* delay tactic, leading to another pointless task until the novel ends at the climax. Sure, there are plenty of "exciting things" happening so it feels as though the novel has a lot going on, but the pace is slow because readers aren't invested in the outcome of those tasks and they don't *care*. They *know* the problem doesn't change anything. Overcoming that obstacle will reveal no new information nor change anything that happens next.

For example, a fallen tree across the road isn't a conflict, though it is an "obstacle in the way." However, a guy in the road with a gun *feels* like it ought to be a strong conflict. The driver wants to pass, the gunman wants to stop her—but it's not a conflict readers are likely to care about if it doesn't do all the things a strong conflict *also* needs to do. It's just a random guy who appears for no reason other than to delay the time it takes for the protagonist to get past this obstacle.

Obstacles *can* work if the whole point of the obstacle is to delay the protagonist so she misses something critical that *does* have larger ramifications. The delay actually causes problems for the protagonist. Had she not been stuck handling that problem, she would have been on time to do whatever she needed to do (but you need to be careful with this, or too many of the novel's conflicts don't actually mean anything to the story).

This is why "stuff in the way" doesn't hold a reader's interest, even though it technically might seem as though there's conflict in that scene. It's the challenge to choose the *right* path that turns a "something in the way" obstacle into a conflict that needs a resolution.

Ways to Create Conflict in Your Manuscript

Even though the many layers and different aspects of conflict can be confusing, they do have one great advantage for writers—they provide us multiple options for adding or strengthening the conflict in our novels. We're not limited to one type that every plot needs to adhere to, or one set character arc that always unfolds the same way. We get to mix and match and develop conflicts however they work best with our stories.

Here are ten different ideas for creating conflict.

Think Like a Villain

Conflict is the challenge, struggle, and opposition facing the protagonist, so thinking like the bad guy puts us in the right mindset to be that opposition.

Writers typically spend more time thinking about what the protagonist will do and how she'll get out of trouble and less about how she gets into that trouble in the first place. There's nothing wrong with that, it's just good plotting, but *not* considering the antagonist's side can lead to scenes that go directly to the planned outcome and skip opportunities for conflict.

For example, when I was working on a scene for my second novel, *Blue Fire*, I found myself with a scene I knew wasn't strong, even though it should have been. My protagonist, Nya, had to break into and out of a prison and fight a bunch of bad guys. I knew when I started the scene that she got away, but it needed to be a tough fight. The problem: Since I knew she'd escape, I had her acting to achieve *that* goal, and the scene unfolded as if escaping was an inevitable conclusion. So instead of it being a tough fight, it felt too easy. I knew something was wrong. Then it hit me...

The conflict wasn't about how Nya *escaped*, it was about how the bad guys tried to *stop* her from escaping. The conflict was in the challenge she faced trying to achieve her goal.

Once I flipped sides and looked at the scene through the bad guy's perspective, it all fell into place. These poor guards were just doing their jobs and this girl was busting into their prison to free some of their prisoners. This was bad for them. What would they do to stop her? What contingencies did they already have in place to handle potential prison breaks?

After imagining the same conflict from the guards' perspective it was much easier to create the challenges Nya had to face and overcome to rescue her friends. Just to be clear, I didn't actually *write* the scene from their perspective, I only thought about what they'd do to stop her and then had her encounter those things.

Let's go through this step-by-step with a different example:

Bob, Jane, and Sally are all survivors on the run during a zombie apocalypse. They're trapped in a Denny's, with zombies all around them. They need to get out before they're the ones on the lunch menu.

Traditionally, we'd examine the scene and look for potential obstacles to cause trouble (conflict).

Let's imagine zombies are covering all the exits. They're bashing themselves against the doors and windows and the glass is going to break any time now. Maybe Sally and Jane have differing opinions on what to do and are arguing, making it hard to focus or get everyone to work together.

What's our conflict? The trio wants to escape, the zombies want to prevent them from leaving. The challenge for Bob and the gang is to get past the zombies without anyone getting hurt or eaten.

What are the challenges to the goal of escaping? The zombies. Bob and the gang are low on ammo. The kitchen is on fire. Jane is injured.

With these problems the scene will most likely play out like this: Zombies try to get in, Bob deals with each problem as it occurs. He runs out of ammo, searches for other lethal items, maybe even uses the fire to kill enough zombies to escape. Since we know Bob is going to escape, the scene is more a matter of, "How is Bob going to use these pieces to get out of there?" Because of that, there's no real tension that he *isn't* going to get out of there. The scene is going to unfold as expected, because the zombies are more obstacle than challenge. The conflict is fairly weak.

Right now, the zombies are pretty mindless in this story, so they're more monster than villain. To strengthen this conflict, let's turn them into real bad guys (because that's where the fun is). What if these particular zombies are not the kind Bob has been encountering all along? Maybe these particular zombies came across a secret government safe house and ate some test subjects for a new brain enhancing serum, so now they're *smart* zombies.

These zombies aren't going to just whack their heads on the door until it breaks. They'll have a plan. This will certainly change how Bob acts, but even so, it'll still be along the lines of what Bob has to do to get out, and when we plot this, we'll most likely think about things that Bob can do to achieve that ultimate goal of getting away.

Now flip it.

Think about it from the smart zombies' perspective. What will these zombies do to get into that Denny's so they can eat Bob and the others? Shove dumpsters against the windows to prevent escape? Create a situation where the only possible exit is into a trap they've set? Sacrifice the regular zombies to send the fire deeper into the restaurant and force Bob out? What if these zombies *set* the fire in the first place? If you were a zombie, what would you do to get to these people?

Suddenly it's not just about Bob getting away. It's about Bob having to overcome challenges that aren't so easy to guess the outcome. Failing here is a real possibility, so the tension is jacked high and the conflict feels stronger. Readers don't know what will happen next because anything could. And Bob is going to get a huge shock when zombies aren't acting like he's used to seeing. He'll have to make tougher decisions, because what he's always done won't work anymore. This will add a lot of uncertainty to the scene and raise the tension.

It's the same situation, but this time, we're not plotting for the win we're plotting for the *loss*, and making Bob earn his win by figuring out how to overcome the challenges and making the right choices to succeed. And by thinking like the bad guy for a bit, we're not picking the easy way out. We're creating tough situations that will require some fancy footwork by the protagonist to overcome.

Create stronger conflicts by getting inside the heads of those bad guys and thinking about what they'd do to get what *they* want. You might find yourself saying, "There's no way my protagonist can get out of that," but do it anyway and make her work for it. Because the harder *you* have to think, the harder your *protagonist* has to think, and the more challenging that conflict will be to overcome.

Work Against the Protagonist

Sometimes the protagonist is following along with the plot and doing what she needs to do, and even though things are problematic, there's no sense that there's *really* anything in the way trying to stop her. Sure, it's hard, but she just needs to fight through it to the next step of the plot—classic "stuff in the way" obstacles that aren't true conflicts.

When the protagonist is just mowing down obstacles in the way, add conflict by making her do what she *doesn't* want to do.

Ask the protagonist to go against a personal belief: Create a situation where the "right" answer or course of action clearly, absolutely goes against everything the protagonist knows is right and true.

Make the protagonist face a choice she doesn't want to make: Sometimes we have to make decisions we don't like, especially when we know they'll come back to bite us later. Will the protagonist be strong enough to make that choice?

Force the protagonist to make a bad choice: This is one of my favorites, since mistakes are great fodder for plot. The protagonist can act, and that action can cause more trouble than she was trying to prevent in the first place. This works even better if she makes the wrong choice because she's trying to avoid violating a personal belief.

Make the protagonist face an *impossible* choice: Some choices have no good outcomes and the protagonist must choose the lesser of two evils. Maybe the only way to save the child is to let the mother die? No matter what the options are, no matter what the protagonist decides, something horrible will happen—but not deciding is even *worse*.

Let the protagonist fail: This one can be dangerous, so be wary of putting your characters in situations that stop the story, but sometimes failing is an unexpected and compelling path to take. It's not just a setback, it's real failure with real consequences. If those consequences play off an internal conflict or past bad choice, so much the better.

Force the protagonist to do something she'll regret: This works well if what she does early on affects the plot later—a choice she makes trying to avoid a consequence that directly leads to a far worse problem or situation. Maybe she sees this regret coming and has no choice but to do it anyway. Maybe she has no clue what problems she's about to bring down on herself. Or better still, *she* doesn't, but the *reader* does.

Force the protagonist to address an issue she's been avoiding: This is a great conflict for characters who need to learn a lesson and grow. Characters don't always want to face their demons, but they have no choice if you shove those demons in their faces—and the fallout can be devastating.

Don't forget about the other characters who might be working against the protagonist as well. If everyone is on the same page and working as one, you could be missing out on potential areas for conflict.

Let someone actively prevent the protagonist from getting or doing what she wants: Give people reasons not to help your protagonist, such as a clerk who won't tell her what she needs to know, or a guard she can't sneak past. Maybe a minion of the antagonist has a full-on plan of his own to stop her.

Let someone disagree with the protagonist: Even if two people want the same thing, they might have different ideas on how to get it. Give supporting characters other ideas about what the protagonist is doing. Maybe they flat out think she's wrong, or maybe they agree but think she's going about it the wrong way and want to keep her from making a mistake. Even good intentions can create trouble if the person hearing the advice doesn't like it.

Give other characters agendas that interfere with the protagonist's plan: If two guys are after the same girl, one might try to sabotage the other. Or maybe a secondary character thinks she's protecting the protagonist by making sure she fails.

Let characters keep things from the protagonist: Secrets can add a lot of conflict, especially if keeping that secret affects the protagonist or her plans. Even a minor secret that does little more than embarrass a character if she reveals it could affect how that character acts or what she does to support (or not support) the protagonist.

Shift your thinking from, "How do I get my protagonist to the climax?" to, "How can I keep my protagonist from the climax?" and you'll spot all kinds of delightful opportunities to create compelling conflicts in your scenes.

Extra tip: For a lukewarm scene try writing it with the *opposite* outcome instead and see how it works. Sometimes what we *don't* plan is exactly what the scene needs.

Let the Protagonist Want What She Can't Have

A fun way to create internal conflict with external challenges is to let the protagonist want something that's not good for her.

I call it the Halloween Candy Principle.

Every year, millions of kids go trick or treating and bring home buckets of candy. What they want is to eat it in huge quantities. What's best for them is to eat a few pieces at a time. The conflict is, "I want to eat a pound of candy, but it will make me sick." And thus, vast sums of kids do what they want and get sick every year. Those who learn not to eat too much the first day get to enjoy the candy for months. Those who don't, get sick a few times and the candy is taken away.

If this was a scene it would look like this:

The goal: To eat lots of candy.

The stakes: Gut-wrenching pain and nausea, loss of treasured candy.

The conflict: Risk pain to eat candy.

Each kid has to face the hard choice of satisfying that urge to gorge or prevent sickness and candy loss.

Great story conflict can come from the protagonist doing what she knows is going to have unpleasant consequences because she *wants* to do it. It's the choice to act in spite of the risks that makes it interesting.

Let your protagonist want things that are bad for her (even if that "bad" thing ultimately gets her what's good for her in the end).

Look at the conflict in your current manuscript:

State the goal: What does your protagonist want?

Your protagonist will want many things throughout the course of the novel. Some of them will be small goals to drive a scene, others will be the larger core conflict goals that are the reason the book exists. No matter what the scope of that problem is, the structure is the same— protagonist has a goal and works to resolve that goal, overcoming the challenges preventing her from achieving her goal along the way.

State the stakes: What happens to your protagonist personally if she doesn't get that want?

Look for a consequence akin to getting sick from candy (only on a scale to match your story). It's personal, it's a direct result of what the protagonist does, and it's something she doesn't want to have happen to her because it's horrible, or it might cause worse problems (like losing the candy).

State the conflict: What does your protagonist want that is "bad" for her?

"Bad" is subjective. It's "bad" because it will cause pain before it brings happiness (or as in our candy example, it will cause brief happiness before pain and thus risk ongoing happiness). If the want was truly bad for the protagonist, odds are it wouldn't be the point of the novel. But to get that ultimate want (be it to escape a situation, prevent an injustice, find love, or be happy) there will be hard choices to make and prices to pay. If it was easy and cost nothing, it wouldn't be a story-worthy problem.

If your protagonist doesn't want *anything* that's bad for her, that's a red flag that you have low or missing conflict in the scene. Characters need to face tough choices and make sacrifices by the end of the novel. The conflict comes from the struggle to get what they want, even though it's hard (if they ration the candy they can enjoy it for months).

Look for the story equivalent of Halloween candy in your scenes and let your characters make the hard choice to eat or not to eat.

Put the Protagonist's Needs and Wants at Odds

When the conflict is focused on getting the external goal only, then what is thrown in the protagonist's path is just a delay tactic, no matter how amazing the path to get there is. We might enjoy seeing those obstacles overcome, but without the protagonist facing tough challenges that require tougher choices, there's no *actual* personal conflict.

While this can work in a movie (*Raiders of the Lost Ark* is probably the best-known example here), it tends to feel shallow in a novel. Action is quite compelling visually, but it has less impact when described. The emotional side is typically more compelling in written form (maybe that's why love letters are so effective).

Let's look at an example:

In my novel, *The Shifter*, my protagonist Nya wants to find (and later save) her sister, Tali. That's her goal and what she wants. But what she *needs* is freedom—the literal "not be oppressed by the occupying army" type, as well as the "free to be who I really am" type. In most aspects of her life she's trapped, and that's the theme of the novel.

So naturally, the conflict in finding Tali is Nya having to do the one thing that is guaranteed to make every bad guy in the land want to kidnap her and trap her forever.

What she *wants* (to save her sister) conflicts with what she *needs* (to be free). Having one means she loses the other, and she's not willing to give up on her sister. But to win, she has to embrace who she is and use it to save Tali (and herself). Until she becomes who she truly is, she'll never be free (her character arc). To become who she truly is, she has to risk that freedom.

Of course, she doesn't realize this at the start of the series, as needs can be unconscious goals. She knows she wants to be free of what's trapping her, but she has no idea what will actually make her free. She has to undergo the trials of the plot to figure that out, which also creates her character arc.

Needs can be (and often are) unclear for protagonists at the start of a story. What they think will make them happy (the want) isn't what will actually make them happy (the need), but they have no clue what they really need until they get the want and find it lacking.

Most of the smaller scene-driving challenges in the novel are due to the conflict of want versus need. Nya gets caught stealing and wants to escape, and she uses her special pain-shifting ability to do it—which draws attention to her and risks her freedom. She gets plenty of opportunities to be the person she wants to be, but they all come with a price she doesn't want to pay. Sometimes she refuses, sometimes she compromises, and sometimes she pays it, knowing what it will mean later, but also knowing that *not* paying it is the worst option.

This "you can have what you want, but it'll cost you" concept creates personal conflict that makes readers care about the characters and the outcomes of their actions and choices. It creates the story-driving conflict the plot is trying to illustrate. Yes, Nya can save her sister, but she'll have to become the most-wanted girl in two nations to do it. But Nya won't leave family behind so she'll make the sacrifices, even though she fights how much is taken from her every step of the way. Stripping her of her armor and protection (her anonymity) is what eventually reveals the real her, and when that's all she has left, she has no choice but to embrace it.

Which is what readers have been waiting for all along (because Nya can kick some serious butt when she cuts loose).

Look at your current project and ask:

What does your protagonist want? This is the core conflict problem she needs to resolve in the novel. It's what the book's plot is about. Why does she *think* this will make her happy? Will it—why or why not?

What does your protagonist need? This is the character arc. This is what *will* make her happy and allow her to be the person she really wants to be. Is it an unconscious or conscious need?

How do those two things conflict with each other? This is where the actual challenges will lie and where you'll draw much of the conflict from. The other problems in the book are just examples that illustrate this core conflict. The protagonist can't have both goals (need and want), and having one creates a problem with the other.

How does one force her to make sacrifices to have the other? If the protagonist can have both the want and the need without paying a high price, it's not a conflict. What are the downsides to having (and losing) the want versus having (and losing) the need?

If you don't see a clear or strong conflict, brainstorm ways you might add that conflict. Or, look deeper at what your story is *really* about. It's possible you have an inkling of what the protagonist's need is, but you never articulated it. You have a gut feeling you can't quite put into words, but it's guided you so far.

Once you find (or clarify) it, look at your story again. Odds are you'll see scenes that will be much stronger if you add an aspect of that newfound conflict to them. On plot-heavy novels, you might even see the exact character arc you need to make that story sing.

Ask What the *Other* Characters Want

It seems simple, but what often saps the conflict from a scene is that non-point-of-view characters know what the protagonist wants (because the author does) so they just go along with it or don't try all that hard to stop it. Friends of the protagonist are on her side and support whatever she's doing and how she's doing it. Everyone is always on the same page because that's where the plot is going, so even when the bad guys are trying to stop the protagonist, it doesn't always feel like their hearts are in it (like we talked about in "Think Like a Villain").

To create conflict, consider who in the scene might not want what the protagonist wants.

Let's say you're writing a scene with three people at a restaurant—Kate, the protagonist; Robert, the husband; and Brenda, the waitress. Kate and Robert have been having trouble getting along lately and things are strained between them. They're having dinner at the restaurant where Robert proposed years ago. Kate wants to ask Robert to start going to marriage counseling, and by the end of the scene, he'll agree and move the plot forward.

The scene will likely play out with some conflict, as Kate is nervous about asking and Robert will be hesitant and not want to do it right away. This is a scene that will show how these two don't always agree, but maybe there's still hope. It's easy to see how a scene like this could end exactly as Kate wants it to—she gets her way and they go to counseling. The author knows this is where the plot is going and this scene is just a way to get there.

There's also a good chance that this scene won't have a compelling conflict making readers eager to see what happens. Going to counseling is a predictable conclusion (since it's Kate's goal) so they expect it to end that way. They might even be looking ahead already to see what happens once the unhappy couple *gets* to the counselor's office.

But…

What if we forget what Kate wants for a minute and ask what *Robert* wants. And don't just give him a weak goal that helps Kate get her way— give him a real goal that fits who he is and also opposes what Kate wants.

Let's say Robert doesn't want counseling; he wants a divorce.

This is the opposite of what Kate wants, and it gives Robert motivation to oppose Kate's goal. Maybe he's met someone else, or he doesn't like who Kate has become, or he's just tired of trying to be the man she thinks he is all the time. Whatever his reasons, make them personal to him and separate from what Kate wants.

With this conflict the scene takes on a new dynamic, because as we write it, we know exactly why Robert is balking and what he might say to reject Kate's idea. He'll hem and haw, try to talk her out of it, and finally have to either give in and tell her he wants a divorce, or cave in and do what she wants even though it's not what *he* wants. It might even enrich the plot because now the outcome isn't so certain. Even if he agrees to counseling, readers know there's more going on here because of what was revealed (or suggested) in this improved scene.

But let's not forget Brenda, the waitress. What does *she* want?

Brenda wants to get out of work early because she has a final exam the next day she's barely studied for.

This is a minor moment in the big picture of the plot, and honestly, no one will care what Brenda-the-walk-on-character wants. She's a nobody, but she's in the scene and you *can* use her to raise tensions and add conflict by thinking about what she wants and having her act accordingly.

For example:

▶ She might rush them to order, sparking Robert's annoying impatient side that Kate wishes he'd work on.

▶ She might bring Kate's well-done steak out too soon and cause her to send it back, something that always drives Robert crazy.

▶ She might be distracted and let them sit instead of checking back on them, giving them time to remember the night they got engaged and reconsider where they go from here.

▶ She might show up during personal moments of the conversation and make Kate and Robert uncomfortable and back off from being honest about what they want.

Sure, she's a small character, but she has the *ability to put pressure on an already tense situation* and make it harder to overcome the challenges Kate and Robert face.

Knowing what every character in a scene wants doesn't mean you have to explain or reveal that goal to the reader, though. It's a little trick to remind *you* that people act independently of each other, and that applies to novels as well as life. Giving each character something to strive for can add a layer of interest to a scene, and turn a predictable conflict into a compelling one.

Make Characters Make Tough Choices

Choices are big in fiction. Every protagonist faces countless choices in a novel, and the ones that really make her struggle are the ones the reader is going to remember. But as we're plotting our stories, are we remembering to make those choices *tough*?

To put that conflict back in, present challenges that will force the protagonist to make tough choices. You could:

Add internal struggles: Internal conflict is often where the fun stuff happens. Maybe everything about your protagonist wants her to go one way, but she kinda *has* to go the other way to get what she wants. Is she willing to sacrifice something to get her goal? Can you make it harder on the protagonist to know what the right thing to do is? Give the protagonist a choice in how she overcomes the conflict, and make those choices difficult and push her to her limits or out of her comfort zone.

Make the choices hard: A difficult choice is one that has consequences no matter what's chosen. It also allows readers to consider what *they* might do in the same situation, helping them to connect to the character better.

Be careful not to mistake a hard choice with one that only looks hard, but really isn't. If the "right" choice is clear, even though that choice is something that will be hard to do (or hard to deal with), it isn't really a choice. It's just something hard the protagonist has to do.

Make the outcome difficult to predict: No matter how tough the choice, if readers can see it coming it won't keep them all that engaged (unless it's something they've dreaded coming and see it barreling down on them). Make sure there's some mystery to which way the story will go, and there's not a direct line from what the protagonist wants to what she needs to do to get it.

Write yourself into a corner: Although it can be scary, sometimes the best thing we can do is write ourselves into a corner (where even *we* don't know how the protagonist will get out of the problem). It forces us to think outside the plot and focus on what would be best for the scene based on what's happening in that scene.

If your protagonist *is* facing tough choices and the conflict still feels weak, it might not be the choice itself that's the problem, but the stakes in making that choice.

Tough Choices Need Strong Stakes

A choice is only as hard as the consequence for failing to make the right choice, so consider the stakes the protagonist is risking.

For example, readers are more likely to care about a father trying not to let his four-year-old daughter down on her birthday than a police officer who's trying to save the city from a terrorist. Seeing the tears in the child's eyes, knowing how much she wants her daddy to be there, watching the father struggle to make it—all of these things are personal and relatable and tug at a reader's heartstrings. But millions of people dying and a guy trying to stop it because it's his job doesn't affect us the same emotionally (though it might pique reader interest from an intellectual perspective—which is why genre matters to conflict).

What the protagonist and other characters have at stake determines how well the conflict works. Let's explore the various levels of stakes and how they affect the conflict:

Low Stakes: Low stakes are situations where there is a consequence, but it doesn't change the life of the protagonist all that much. Making a choice doesn't affect the story in any major way, and the end result will be the same regardless of which choice the protagonist makes at that moment.

Common low stakes include situations where a consequence is possible, but when that consequence happens it's not a big deal and nothing actually changes. It also includes decisions where either choice works for the protagonist (it doesn't matter what she does, it still gets her where she wants to go), or decisions where there really *is* only one option—such as one choice leads to certain death, the other to victory. Yes, there are choices to be made with low stakes, and those choices may actually move the plot forward a little, but they're not making readers worry about the outcome so the conflict is weak.

For example:

▶ A young girl is spying on her brother, but getting caught just gets her yelled at and nothing comes of it.

▶ A detailed plan to break into the antagonist's lair unfolds without a single problem.

▶ A choice between two potential romantic partners—and either could make the protagonist happy.

Medium Stakes: Medium stakes occur in situations where the consequence will change the life of the protagonist, but not in any long-lasting way. The stakes have an effect on the bigger story, and will probably make things a bit tougher, but failing isn't going to change the protagonist that dramatically in the long term. These stakes are often fun and a little exciting as they can make the individual scenes more interesting. It's not about worrying if the protagonist will win, but how this choice is going to make things worse down the road.

Common medium stakes include situations where readers care about the outcome, and that outcome will cause a change in how the protagonist moves forward from this point. Making a mistake has larger ramifications and the protagonist can usually see what the risks are and must decide if they're worth it or not. They also include choices where the protagonist knowingly makes things tougher for the sake of achieving something that matters more, such as risking capture to rescue a friend.

For example:

> ▶ A young girl is spying on her brother, who plans to rob the local gas station with his friends. Getting caught could cause her personal problems *with* her sibling, but revealing what she knows could create even bigger problems *for* her sibling.

> ▶ A detailed plan to break into the antagonist's lair requires the characters to separate, and odds are high that not everyone will make it out alive.

> ▶ A choice between two potential romantic partners—one can provide the protagonist with the financial and emotional stability she needs, and the other can offer her the passion and excitement she craves.

High Stakes: High-stakes situations have consequences that will severely change the protagonist's life. The decisions made have far-reaching consequences and failing here will change who that protagonist is.

Common high stakes include situations where failing will shake the protagonist to her core and cause long-lasting personal damage (either physical, mental, or emotional). They also include choices where the protagonist must make a sacrifice about something she cares deeply about, such as choosing to walk away from someone she loves because it's the only way to save his life. It's about how that choice and the consequences of that choice will irrevocably change the protagonist forever.

For example:

> ▶ A young girl agrees to help her brother rob a gas station with his friends, but plans to stop him before he can do the job.

▶ Breaking into the antagonist's lair to save the best friend requires the protagonist to give up the one item she's spent all novel trying to obtain.

▶ A choice between two potential romantic partners—either can make the protagonist happy, but choosing one means abandoning a lifelong dream, and choosing the other means leaving a family behind. Or the third choice—walking away from both people.

Anything Can Be High or Low Stakes

What makes something high or low stakes is how it affects the protagonist on an emotional level. The smallest, most mundane event can be devastating to the right person in the right circumstance, while the largest, most horrendous event can be just another day at the office to someone commonly facing that threat.

If the stakes matter to the protagonist *and* the reader, the outcome of the choice will also matter.

Let Characters Screw Up Their Decisions

As people, we want to make the right choices, so it's only natural that those are the choices that first come to us as we write. But doing the right thing doesn't always cause wonderful conflict (though when it does it's writing gold). Characters shouldn't act like people who have had three weeks to consider their options just because the author took that long to write the scene. A decision made in the heat of the moment isn't the same as one made with weeks to consider.

Here are some fun ways you can have your characters make the wrong choice next time they're faced with an all-important decision:

Let them be impulsive: This is a helpful flaw for characters who need to learn patience, or who don't always consider how their actions affect others. Snap judgments, quick decisions, charging full-speed ahead without thinking beyond the now. If you need to get your protagonist in over her head fast, consider this mistake.

Let them make a decision under pressure: When you think about it, you should always force your characters to do this, because a ticking clock is a reliable way to raise stakes and increase tensions in a story. Small pressures build to big explosions, so if you need your characters to blow their tops, try looking for small ways to eat at them leading up to that explosion.

Let them over-analyze something: If characters are so busy trying to figure out the right thing to do, they might totally miss the opportunity to act at all. Lost chances a character can regret later make wonderful seeds to plant early on in a story, and can cause huge emotional trauma during that Dark Moment of the Soul at the end of act two. Overanalyzing can also work to sneak in possible dangers and outcomes, helping to raise tensions and keep things unpredictable since so many bad things might occur.

Let them assume they know it all: Perfect for the protagonist who needs to learn a valuable lesson about working with others. Let her be convinced she's right and doesn't need advice from anyone else. The fall here when reality strikes will be devastating and all the more satisfying.

Let them not consider all the options: Choices made without the benefit of a solid foundation of knowledge can lead to a myriad of delightful screw ups. Maybe there's no time for research, or there's something the protagonist just doesn't want to think about (denial, much?). Missing key information can send a character into a mess of their own making.

Let them not ask advice: Who needs a long-winded story from some old geezer about how he did it when he was younger? Times change, and what worked then surely won't work now. This is a flaw for the protagonist who doesn't respect tradition or the counsel of others. The more people she pisses off, the fewer there will be when she needs them at the climax.

Don't let them make alternative plans: Who needs Plan B? An overconfident protagonist might never see the need for backup plans, because everything is going to go just like she expects. So when things start falling to pieces, she's very likely incapable of wise action to correct her mistake. This causes events to snowball, getting her into more and more delicious trouble.

Making smart choices is vital in the real world, but making conflict-creating bad choices is a must for the fictional world. While you don't want your characters to be stupid (unless it's by design), try adding a few bad decision-making moments to your characters and enjoy the fun.

Cause Trouble Without Making Trouble

Smaller, quieter conflicts can add challenges to a scene without turning it into a big, melodramatic mess. They're especially good for character-driven novels where the focus is more internal than external, but they also work well for internal goals and character arcs in a plot-driven novel.

Anything that gets in the way of what the protagonist wants to do is a potential conflict to develop. These quiet moments also give you a chance to examine multiple sides of an issue without it coming across as preaching or infodumping. Two characters having an honest debate can share a lot of information in a natural way that fits the story and flows seamlessly into the narrative.

The key to non-violent trouble is people with different wants. You want to take a nap after a long day, your kids want to play Monopoly with you. What you want is in conflict with what they want. But this isn't going to turn into a battle, and there's no bad guy here. Just two sides who both want something different.

Here are some ways to create problems without putting your protagonist's life in danger:

Make her balk: She who hesitates is lost. Not acting at the right moment can cause all kinds of trouble. And then there's that lovely guilt and second guessing you can play with later.

Blow her mind: Discovering something shocking that changes the protagonist's worldview can send her into a tailspin. Having her world turned upside down can affect her judgment, her belief system, or her very self-image. When everything is off kilter, anything can happen.

Let her be wrong: We all make mistakes. A flawed protagonist who screws up and has to fix it is a great plot tool. The protagonist might need to win in the end, but until then, she can mess up a lot.

Let her be right: Have you ever lied to someone and they called your bluff? The protagonist can call a bluff, too, and then cause worse trouble than if she'd just let it go. Embarrassing someone she'll later need help from will cause trouble for sure.

Let characters disagree: Disagreements make folks dig in their heels even if they're not ready to break out the heavy weapons. For example, Mom sends her daughter back upstairs to change out of a too-sexy outfit, even though the daughter *really* wants to wear it. Your boss makes the protagonist work over the weekend when she has other plans. These aren't life-shattering issues, but if the mother and daughter already have a strained relationship, this simple conflict could ignite that larger fuse. And if your protagonist is already in hot water over working too hard, another missed weekend could end in divorce.

Let her try to avoid hurt feelings: Some conflicts stem from love or friendship. For example, the protagonist wants to go to a party, but her best friend wasn't invited. If she goes, she'll hurt her friend's feelings. Hurting someone's feelings is a great conflict that might have huge repercussions later on when the character *needs* that friend to be there. They're also a wonderful way to mirror a larger emotional issue or show a character's growth (or the need to grow). Since these are personal, the stakes are naturally higher even if the conflict is mundane. No one wants to hurt someone they care about.

Let things get competitive: Rivalries and friendly competition can cause conflicts, especially if they start out friendly then turn more serious. Even a playful one-upmanship rivalry can make readers curious to see what happens between those characters. Who will get the upper hand this time? Will there ever be a moment when that upper hand matters? They're even handy to show a skill the character might need later on without shoving it in the reader's face.

Find the humor in the conflict: Some conflicts can be all about the funny, like Mom trying to put a diaper on a toddler who's running around laughing. Their goals are in opposition (Mom wants a diapered baby, baby wants to be naked and free) but there's nothing adversarial here. While funny conflicts probably won't work all the time (there's often little to no stakes in this type) they can add enjoyable levity and work well with more serious moments. A light scene right after a dark scene can be the calm breather readers need before everything breaks loose. It can give your character something to do if the scene is mostly dialogue and feels static. A funny conflict that distracts your protagonist might allow her to miss something she'll need later. Or the funny conflict might just be a way to share some aspect of your protagonist and make readers like and care about her—very useful for opening scenes.

A little goes a long way, so don't feel you have to add a ton of challenges to every single scene. If it takes seventeen steps to get a glass of milk from the fridge, you might be piling on the conflicts a little thick—just sprinkle them in where they'd have the most impact.

Non-violent conflict is wondering what decisions the characters will make or how they'll react to something profound. It's not the literary equivalent of special effects; it's about wondering what a character will do.

Add Small Problems to Your Plot

When you're creating your characters and their lives, don't forget to add in the little things that can cause them trouble, even if it's not earth-shattering trouble. Think about the bad days you've had, where nothing went right, and how that escalated into you snapping and yelling at someone who didn't deserve it. Or caused you to do something you wouldn't have ordinarily done had you not already been stressed by stupid little things.

In other words, pile on the problems.

For example, in *The Shifter*, finding food and work is a small problem my protagonist has to deal with every day. It's not a major event in the book, but it does cause her extra trouble, and it does start her down the path that becomes the major conflict of the story. It's also something that can add a layer of difficulty to everything she does. Life is hard for her, even the simple everyday things. A hard life makes everything more difficult.

Places to look for conflict:

World building: What inherent problems occur in this character's world?

Work: What problem issues can come up on the job?

Family: Are there any family issues that can throw a wrench in the protagonist's plan?

Friends: Can a friend come to them for help at a bad time?

Health: Is there a medical issue that can cause recurring trouble?

Sometimes in our stories, we need our characters to act in ways contrary to what the average person would do. Take a chance, make a bad choice, be reckless or mean. A bad day can go a long way toward shoving someone in the right (meaning wrong) direction.

Add pressure prior to a big turning point: Small conflicts can put the protagonist in the wrong mindset during a major turning point. Find those moments that need extra conflict and go back a few scenes (or even chapters). Look for places where the protagonist's day/goal/problem would be made a little bit worse by one more thing going wrong.

Strengthen slow scenes by adding additional problems: Slow scenes can benefit from added small problems, so check any spots that drag and look for ways to make things a little more difficult. These could be good spots to add those pressure points.

Add conflict with the emotions: Emotional situations or turning points can be made more powerful by a small issue or conflict that underlines or further illustrates that emotion—or is completely contrary to it. What might happen if the protagonist had to fake being happy when she wanted to curl up and cry?

Be wary of tossing in a small issue just to add a small issue, though. Empty problems will read like "stuff in the way" and make the book feel full of random obstacles without a real plot or story.

When you add a small problem, make sure it creates the right pressure to cause conflict in the scene. It might:

- Put stress on an existing problem

- Add a ticking clock

- Push an emotional button

- Take advantage of a character flaw and bring it to light

- Undermine the character so they're in bad shape for the next problem

- Raise the stakes

- Provide an opportunity for the protagonist to fail

- Provide an opportunity for the protagonist to learn a skill they'll need later

Things happen in our lives all the time, so it makes sense to let our characters experience that same chaos and uncertainty that will make everything they do a little more challenging.

Take Advantage of the Environment

We all know *what* happens in a story is important, but as we saw earlier, *where* it happens can have a profound effect on the characters and how they resolve their conflicts as well. If your setting doesn't add something to the story, you're wasting a great opportunity to deepen your novel or layer in more conflicts.

A solid example of how setting can affect the conflict of a novel is the movie *District 9*. In the movie, a ship full of aliens are space-wrecked on Earth and have spent the past twenty years living in a controlled area called *District 9*. Naturally, the aliens and the humans have difficulty living and playing well together and conflict ensues.

One of the things I found most interesting about this movie was the choice of setting. The alien ship could have settled over any city, but the writers chose Johannesburg, South Africa. I think that the events depicted in the film would not have happened the same way had this been set in, say, Los Angeles, Chicago, or London. The setting brought a cultural history to the problem that made it very believable for things to have happened as they did. Since South Africa has a history with racial strife and apartheid, attitudes toward the aliens were strongly affected by that past. In this case, it wasn't an issue of race, but of species. What happened in the movie fits very well with the history of the setting.

Setting also played a big role in *The Shifter*. Many of the problems Nya faces are directly related to the fact that her city is under enemy occupation. Her attitude about nearly everything is colored by this fact and her experiences with this. Were I to move the setting, the book would lose many of its more interesting aspects. The layers of conflict and meaning wouldn't be there anymore, and those layers are critical to the story.

Here are some ways to use the environment to create or deepen the conflict:

Choose the worst setting for the protagonist to face her challenge: Walking through a clean room isn't hard, but walking through a room strewn with broken glass or ten thousand LEGO bricks is a lot more problematic. What about your setting might affect the conflicts in your novel?

Use the setting to push the protagonist out of her comfort zone: Fighting for your life in the dark when you're afraid of the dark makes it even harder to keep your cool. The setting can make the protagonist physically or emotionally uncomfortable, which can make her less capable of handling the challenge at hand.

Let the setting give the antagonist the advantage: It's much easier to gain the upper hand when you're familiar with the terrain. Setting a scene in a location that works for the antagonist adds another layer of difficulty to the task.

Use the setting to put the protagonist at a disadvantage: Even small disadvantages can add up and put the right pressures on a character. Narrow hallways can limit a large or agile protagonist. Cold might cause trouble for the protagonist who isn't dressed appropriately for the weather. Having to defend yourself while wearing high heels at a party can even be a problem (though it could turn out to be the solution if you use the heels as a weapon).

Let the location enhance the thematic elements of the conflict: If your characters are worried about how they're going to pay the rent and how their latest get-rich scheme failed, letting them discuss this as they're walking through a poor neighborhood gives you opportunities to show the poverty-stricken world and reinforce what they have to lose if they can't come up with the money.

Let the location illustrate a character's state of mind: If they're happy, a park or beach might help reflect that. Or you could even use something traditionally dark and gloomy to contrast against their happiness (and vice versa). Someone who is scared might see dangers all around them and give you an opportunity to show the lurking troubles inherent in their world. You can also use that setting to reinforce the emotion you want the reader to feel.

Deepen your conflicts by putting your protagonist into an unlikely or difficult environment. Where we are definitely influences how we feel and what we do.

Go Cause Trouble!

Congratulations! You made it.

Many writers have struggled with creating compelling conflicts in their novels, and I hope this in-depth analysis has given you new insights into how to create conflict in your stories. Often, all it takes is a small push or a slight tweak to an existing situation to bring out the conflict and deepen the scene. Take the tools and the lessons learned here and find the hidden gems scattered throughout your novel.

If you've found this book helpful, please share with friends or leave reviews on your favorite sites.

Most of all, best of luck and good writing!

Janice Hardy
August 2017

Thanks!

Thank you for reading *Understanding Conflict (And What It* Really *Means)*, the second book in my Skill Builders series. I hope you found it useful!

- Reviews help other readers find books. I appreciate all reviews, whether positive or negative.

- If you enjoyed this book, look for the other book in my Skill Builders series, *Understanding Show, Don't Tell (And* Really *Getting It)*, available in paperback and e-book.

- Books in my Foundations of Fiction series include *Plotting Your Novel: Ideas and Structure* and the *Plotting Your Novel Workbook* and my Revising Your Novel series: *Fixing Your Character & Point-of-View Problems, Fixing Your Plot & Story Structure Problems,* and *Fixing Your Setting & Description Problems,* available in paperback and e-book.

- I even write fantasy adventures for teens and adults. My teen novels include The Healing Wars trilogy: *The Shifter, Blue Fire,* and *Darkfall* from Balzer+Bray/HarperCollins, available in paperback, e-book, and audio book formats. As J.T. Hardy, I write fantasy novels for adults, available in paperback and e-book formats.

- **Would you like more writing tips and advice?** Visit my writing site, Fiction University at Fiction-University.com, or follow me on Twitter at @Janice_Hardy.

- **Want to stay updated on future books, workshop, or events?** Subscribe to my newsletter. As a thank you, you'll receive my book, *25 Ways to Strengthen Your Writing Right Now.*

More from Janice Hardy

Award-winning author Janice Hardy (and founder of the popular writing site, Fiction University) takes you inside the writing process to show you how to craft compelling fiction: In her Foundations of Fiction series, she guides you through plotting, developing, and revising a novel. In her Skill Builders series, she uses in-depth analysis and easy-to-understand examples to examine the most common craft questions writers struggle with.

Understanding Show, Don't Tell (And** Really **Getting It) looks at one of the most frustrating aspects of writing—showing, and not telling. Learn what *show, don't tell* means, how to spot told prose in your writing, and when telling is the *right* thing to do. The book also explores aspects of writing that aren't technically telling, but are connected to told prose and can make prose feel told, such as infodumps, description, and backstory.

Understanding Conflict (And What It** Really **Means) looks at how to develop and create conflict in your fiction, and discusses the misconceptions about conflict that confuse and frustrate so many writers. The book also helps you understand what conflict really is, discusses the various aspects of conflict, and reveals why common advice on creating conflict doesn't always work.

Plotting Your Novel: Ideas and Structure shows you how to find and develop stories from that first spark of inspiration to the complete novel. It walks you through how to develop the right characters, find your setting, create your plot, as well as teach you how to identify where your novel fits in the market, and if your idea has what it takes to be a series. Ten self-guided workshops help you craft a solid plot. Each workshop builds upon the other to flesh out your idea as much or as little as you need to start writing, and contains guidance for plotters, pantsers, and everyone in between.

Plotting Your Novel Workbook is the companion guide to *Plotting Your Novel: Ideas and Structure* for those who like a hardcopy approach with easy-to-use worksheets. Its larger workbook format is perfect for writers who enjoy brainstorming on paper and developing their novels in an organized and guided format. No more searching for ideas jotted down on bits of paper. No more losing notes just when you need them most. With more than 100 exercises for the novel-planning process, you can keep all your thoughts in one handy place.

Fixing Your Character & Point-of-View Problems takes you step-by-step through revising character and character-related issues, such as two-dimensional characters, inconsistent points of view, excessive backstory, stale dialogue, didactic internalization, and lack of voice. She'll show you how to analyze your draft, spot any problems or weak areas, and fix those problems. Five self-guided workshops show you how to craft compelling characters, solid points of view, and strong character voices readers will love.

Fixing Your Plot & Story Structure Problems guides you through plot and story structure-related issues, such as wandering plots; a lack of scene structure; no goals, conflicts, or stakes; low tension; no hooks; and slow pacing. She'll show you how to analyze your draft, spot any problems or weak areas, and fix those problems. Five self-guided workshops show you how to craft gripping plots and novels that are impossible to put down.

Fixing Your Setting & Description Problems focuses on setting and description-related issues, such as weak world building, heavy infodumping, told prose, awkward stage direction, inconsistent tone and mood, and overwritten descriptions. She'll show you how to analyze your draft, spot any problems or weak areas, and fix those problems. Five self-guided workshops show you how to craft immersive settings and worlds that draw readers into your story and keep them there.

Acknowledgments

As always, this book would not be here without the help and support of some amazing people.

Huge hugs and thanks to everyone who helped me wrangle this book into shape. My critique partners, Ann and Bonnie; my beta readers, Connie, Joan, Lisa, Peggy, and Trisha; my awesome proofreader, Dori. So many pairs of sharp eyes caught the things I missed, and your inquisitive minds asked some fantastic questions that made this a better book. You guys are the best.

Thank you all.

About the Author

Janice Hardy is the founder of Fiction University, a site dedicated to helping writers improve their craft. She writes both fiction and nonfiction.

Her nonfiction books include the Skill Builders series: *Understanding Show, Don't Tell (And Really Getting It)* and *Understanding Conflict (And What It Really Means)*, and the Foundations of Fiction series: *Plotting Your Novel: Ideas and Structure*, a self-guided workshop for planning or revising a novel; its companion guide, *Plotting Your Novel Workbook*; and the *Revising Your Novel: First Draft to Finished Draft* series.

She's also the author of the teen fantasy trilogy The Healing Wars, including *The Shifter, Blue Fire*, and *Darkfall*, from Balzer+Bray/Harper Collins. *The Shifter* was chosen by the Georgia Center for the Book for its 2014 list of "Ten Books All Young Georgians Should Read." It was also shortlisted for the Waterstones Children's Book Prize (2011) and The Truman Award (2011).

Janice lives in Central Florida with her husband, one yard zombie, two cats, and a very nervous freshwater eel.

Visit her author's site at janicehardy.com for more information, or visit fiction-university.com to learn more about writing.

Follow her at @Janice_Hardy for writing links.

Made in the USA
Lexington, KY
02 July 2018